CND SCRAPBOOK

CND
SCRAPBOOK

JOAN RUDDOCK

OPTIMA

To Keith, who sustained me throughout these years, and to the thousands of activists who sustain the movement.

An OPTIMA book

© Joan Ruddock 1987

First published in 1987 by
Macdonald Optima, a division of
Macdonald & Co. (Publishers) Ltd

A BPCC PLC company

British Library Cataloguing in Publication Data

Ruddock, Joan
    CND scrapbook.
    1. Campaign for Nuclear Disarmament –
    History
    I. Title
    327.1'74'0941   JX1908.G8C3
    ISBN 0-356-14019-9

Macdonald & Co. (Publishers) Ltd
3rd Floor
Greater London House
Hampstead Road
London NW1 7QX

Typesetting by Poole Typesetting (Wessex) Ltd., Bournemouth
Printed and bound in Great Britain by
R. J. Acford, Chichester, Sussex

INTRODUCTION

Over the past six years, I must have wished, a thousand times, that I could write a diary. Indeed, several publishers approached me on the assumption that I had. But such was the pressure of events that I regularly dropped exhausted into bed, incapable of recording a single thought, let alone the day's events. My interest was easily aroused, therefore, when Philippa Stewart proposed that we produce a scrapbook of pictures, highlighting CND's activities past and present.

Despite a full-time job, continuing duties as a vice-chair of CND and involvement in a lengthy and hotly contested selection for a parliamentary seat, I could not resist the commission. Predictably, it has been both a labour of love and an exercise in tremendous frustration. I was always short of time, but then, more time only meant finding more photographs and making even more difficult choices. I didn't want to stop, either, because even as our deadline approached (December 1986) I knew of at least a dozen forthcoming events – not least the general election – which would produce new milestones for CND. But that is as it should be – the day when we can write the final chapter on Britain's disarmament movement is still a long way off.

For me, personally, these past years have been packed, not just with frenetic activity but with drama, crisis and emotion. I cannot count the committees, the meetings, the train journeys, the demonstrations, the letters, the press calls or even those moments when I paused, in amazement, at the strength and vitality of our vast movement. Few people can have been more privileged than Bruce Kent and me, at the centre of CND during the great international resurgence of anti-nuclear activity. We were part of a powerful network of officers, past officers, staff and executive members who tried to put the policies of the annual conference and national council into effect on a daily basis. Yet not many of these people are featured in the book – at events, their responsibility for equipment, stewarding, security, press, money and much more kept them out of the camera's eye.

I have tried to chart the main events in the national life of CND and to give a glimpse of the other major preoccupations of peace activists, namely the Greenham Common Women's Camp, and locally-based group activities. It is also, of course, particularly in the later years, something of a personal view. I hope it will enable supporters, whether featured or not, to share my pride and wonder at the diversity, creativity and energy of a movement that has survived for 30 years and become a major force in British politics. I hope too it will help those who, like me, came late to the movement, to appreciate the long history of struggle by CND and its antecedents. Most of all I hope the book will fall into the hands of those who have not supported us in the past, but may yet be inspired to do so.

Joan Ruddock
1987

THE BEGINNINGS

The world's first atomic test was carried out by the United States at Alamogordo in the New Mexico desert, on 16th July 1945. Within a month two atomic bombs had been used in war – at Hiroshima on August 6th, and at Nagasaki on August 9th.

Opposition to atomic weapons by the few who understood their potential began even before they were used. Most of the atomic scientists had been motivated in their research by the fear that Nazi Germany might be developing an A-bomb. But when, in May 1945, the European war ended and it was clear no such device existed, many saw no further need for the programme. Thus the decision to use the bomb was a controversial one even among those most intimately concerned.

Secrecy has surrounded all nuclear developments, whether in war or peace, and regardless of political system. In Britain the Attlee government, deprived in the postwar years of US nuclear co-operation, decided without any democratic debate to develop its own nuclear weapons. The first Windscale pile, loaded with uranium fuel fabricated at Springfields, became operational in July 1950. On 3rd October 1952, Britain exploded its first atomic bomb off the north-west coast of Australia.

Meanwhile, Europe had become engulfed in the 'cold war', and the Berlin crisis provided the opportunity for a show of force by US bombers on 'temporary' station at British air-bases. Unknown to the British public this was part of a secret agreement made in the summer of 1946 for the emergency use of British bases for a nuclear attack against the Soviet Union. When the bombers arrived in Britain in 1948, the US Defence Secretary recorded in his diary that, once sent, the planes would soon become an accepted fixture.

The North Atlantic Treaty Organization (NATO) was formed in April 1949, and in September the Soviet Union exploded its first atomic bomb. Nine months later war broke out in Korea, and on 30th November 1950, President Truman threatened to use atomic weapons against the Chinese and Korean communists. The nuclear arms race had begun in earnest.

ORGANIZED PROTEST

The first petition against nuclear weapons was drafted by atomic scientist Leo Szilard, and signed by many of his colleagues. It urged the US government not to use the atomic bomb against the Japanese without prior demonstration and without the opportunity for them to surrender. But the public were not to know – the contents of the petition were officially declared 'secret'.

Scientists were also prominent among Britain's early anti-nuclear protestors, as were writers, lawyers and members of the clergy. In April 1950, 100 Cambridge scientists petitioned the government in an attempt to halt the British development of nuclear weapons. Later that same year, on the anniversary of the Hiroshima bombing, Lord Soper preached disarmament to 3,000 members of religious organizations who had assembled in Trafalgar Square.

The first campaign directly involving the public appears to have been organized by the British Peace Committee, which was chaired by Dr J. G. Crowther, a scientist, and included among its members the Dean of Canterbury, Dame Sybil Thorndike and Professors J. D. Bernal and J. B. S. Haldane. The committee collected one million signatures on a petition for the Stockholm Peace Appeal, but their allegiance to the Communist-dominated World Peace Committee drew bitter criticism, and the Labour Party announced that membership of the Peace Committee was incompatible with membership of the party.

Over the next few years anti-nuclear initiatives began to multiply, ranging from direct actions by a small group at the War Office and Aldermaston in 1952, to the launch of the H-bomb National Campaign in 1954. Subsequent campaigns were much influenced by the first US test of a hydrogen bomb in the Pacific, in March 1954. Fallout from the test not only affected hundreds of Marshall Islanders (who had no effective public voice) but 23 sailors on the fishing vessel *Lucky Dragon.* When the boat docked in Japan two weeks later, the whole crew were suffering from radiation sickness, and within six months one had died.

In July 1955 Bertrand Russell drafted an appeal, co-signed by Albert Einstein, in the name of eleven prominent scientists, nine of whom were Nobel laureates. It called upon scientists worldwide to work for peace. This provided the impetus for the international Pugwash conference, still taking place today.

Less famous people were also taking action. In March 1955, Gertrude Fishwick started the Golders Green Campaign Against Nuclear Weapons. Similar local initiatives followed, and in 1957 the National Committee for the Abolition of Nuclear Weapons Tests was formed. Two months later came the formation of the Emergency Committee for Direct Action against Nuclear War.

During the summer of 1957, anti-nuclear activists mobilized within the Labour Party, forming a new Labour H-bomb Campaign Committee and organizing a September rally of 4,000 people in Trafalgar Square. This was a curtain-raiser for the party's struggle for unilateral nuclear disarmament, which was set to dominate that year's party conference – and to continue to do so for very many years.

The foundations of CND were laid in the closing months of 1957. Kingsley Martin, editor of the *New Statesman,* proposed a meeting to discuss starting a mass movement against nuclear weapons. The key people brought together at the home of Canon John Collins, the following January, included Bertrand Russell, Michael Foot, James Cameron and (from the National Committee for the Abolition of Nuclear Weapons Tests – NCANWT) Arthur Goss, Sheila Jones and Peggy Duff.

The NCANWT agreed to transfer its three staff members, offices and files to the new organization – the Campaign for Nuclear Disarmament. A launch meeting was arranged for 17th February 1958, and the new executive committee gave its blessing to a four-day march to Aldermaston. Gerald Holtom designed a symbol for the march, and this later became synonymous with CND in Britain, and recognized worldwide.

Nuclear
Are I
What the Armed For

Sanity

MONTHLY PAPER OF THE CAMPAIGN FOR NUCLEAR DISARMAMENT

JANUARY 1961

1961 – A HAPPIER
NEW YEAR . . . . ?

r fear and detest
h as the

COAST TO COAST CA

IN
James
MYTH

Wayla
BREA

Alder

YOUTH
AGAINST
THE
BOMB

SIXPENCE

CITY PRICES

450 ships,

KENN
GUN

NOV./DEC. 1962—VOLUME 4—NUMBER SIX — MONTHLY JOUR

YOUR
COUNTRY

Sanity
VOICE OF CND

AUGUST 1986

Number 8

WE CAN'T
AFFORD TO
BUILD IT.

WE COULD

NEVER

AFFORD

No 1
Jan 1987
85p

SANITY
FOR A
NUCLEAR-FREE
WORLD

Hiroshim
Pacific

Dave Allen talks

• phone

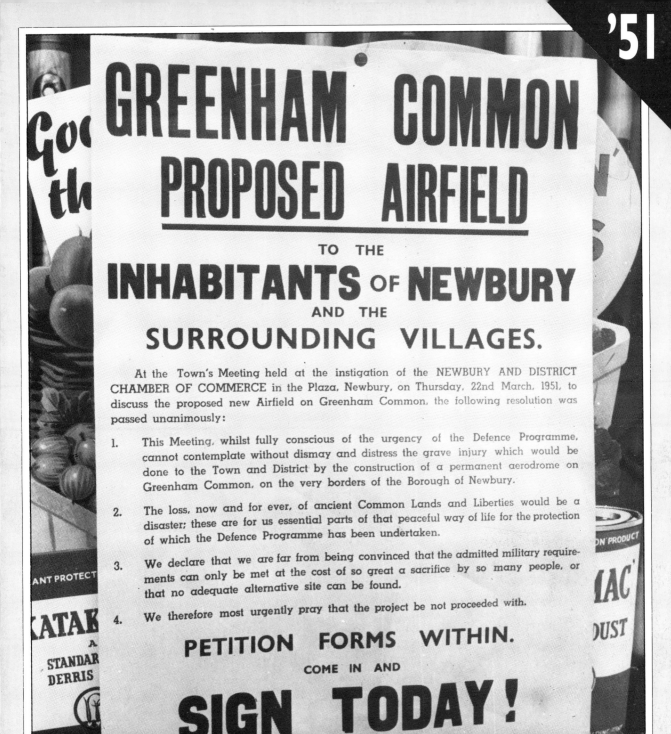

Above Greenham Common, a name which was to hit the headlines repeatedly in the 1980s, was the centre of local controversy as long ago as 1951. The establishment of US bases in Britain began with the Spaatz-Tedder agreement of 1946. By 1950 Lakenheath, Mildenhall, Scampton and Marham had become B-29 bomber bases. Subsequently, under a new 'Ambassador's Agreement', four additional airfields were given to the USAF – Greenham Common, Upper Heyford, Fairford and Brize Norton. The terms of this agreement are still secret.

Above Members of Hampstead Peace Council
protest against a civil defence exercise, November
1953. Successive governments have made plans for
the 'protection' of civilians in the event of nuclear war.
These plans have generally been secret, and the local
authorities charged with implementing them have
been expected to maintain this secrecy. Early plans
included such measures as whitewashing windows if
at home, or jumping into a ditch if caught in the open!

From the beginning, anti-nuclear protesters argued
that no effective protection of civilians could be
provided by a nuclear armed state. In 1954 Coventry
City Council disbanded its Civil Defence committee
on the grounds that it was 'a waste of time and public
money'.

Right In May 1957, 2,000 women marched from
Hyde Park to Trafalgar Square to demonstrate
against Britain's development of the H-bomb. Their
black sashes were inspired by the 'Black Sash'
women's anti-apartheid movement in South Africa.

Women have been involved in the anti-nuclear
movement from the beginning. In 1955 Gertrude
Fishwick, Christian and former suffragette, set up the
Golders Green Committee for the Abolition of
Nuclear Weapons Tests, and this was followed by
many other initiatives by women.

Peace News

No. 1,090   May 17, 1957   4d.   US Air Express Edition 10 cents

The alternative to the H-bomb
UNARMED DEFENCE
Investigate King-Hall's idea
—Barbara Wootton

PROFESSOR BARBARA WOOTTON, Fenner Brockway, MP, Frank Allaun, MP, Anthony Greenwood, MP, and Commander Fox-Pitt, are among the leading British personalities who have in the last week endorsed Commander Sir Stephen King-Hall's call for a serious investigation of the practicality of a new British national defence policy based on reliance on unarmed resistance.

Professor Barbara Wootton, one of the leading British thinkers, writing on page 5, calls Commander King-Hall's proposal "a most significant event."

Growing evidence

Hailing "the fact that a Royal Commission on non-violent resistance has been suggested in responsible quarters," she points out that the history of reform "supports the view that what is ridiculous in one generation, is practical political controversy in the next, and may be realised in the third."

The second and third steps have now "become immensely more likely," she declares, pointing to the "growing body of evidence that organised . . . non-violence has always carried the day where it has been persistently tried."

Non-pacifist Frank Allaun, MP, also writing on page 5, calls Commander King-Hall's statement "the most remarkable, most important, most brilliant, thing I've read for a long time."

> ### BARBARA WOOTTON
> Page five

Scores of MPs are being forced by events, he writes, to the view that violence can achieve nothing, and that a few "have already discussed King-Hall's statement with admiration."

"Timely and justified"

Stuart Morris, Secretary of the Peace Pledge Union, describes the proposals as "of great significance" on page 5, calling the demand "for a full and impartial examination of a fully pacifist policy" both "timely and justified."

He emphasises the need for "a new moral approach" by the British people "which would completely change their own attitude and the whole international situation."

Anthony Greenwood, MP, told Peace News that Commander King-Hall's proposal was "an excellent idea."

● Joining the debate on the proposal next week in Peace News is Lord Altrincham, prominent Conservative spokesman in the House of Lords and Editor of the National and English Review, arguing against Commander King-Hall's proposal. Reginald Thompson, former Daily Telegraph war correspondent and author of "Cry Korea" and Fenner Brockway, MP, both non-pacifists, will write in favour of the call for serious consideration of a national defence policy of unarmed resistance.

Commander King-Hall's article was reproduced in full in last weeks Peace News, copies of which are still available.

A SPOKESMAN OF DANGEROUS INDIVIDUALS
By Peter R. Bell, MA, FLS
Lecturer in Botany, University College London

VISCOUNT CHERWELL, war-time personal assistant to Sir Winston Churchill and a "professional physicist" attacked the campaign against the British H-test when he spoke in the House of Lords on May 8. He considered that Dr. Schweitzer and the Pope, had allowed themselves to be taken in "by the inaccurate propaganda of the friends of Russia.

"I am surprised," he said, "that men in high positions without scientific knowledge or exact information should issue appeals on scientific questions on which they are not competent to judge."

IF a biologist, no matter how eminent, made pronouncements with every show of authority about the detailed structure of atoms, he would justifiably be regarded with some scorn by physicists. This does not deter Lord Cherwell, whose speciality might be described as Engineering Physics, from posing as one qualified to assess the biological dangers of radiation.

Indeed, the very assurance with which he belittled these dangers in his notorious speech in the House of Lords, so different from the cautious and tentative conclusions which were drawn in the report of the Medical Research Council's Committee, indicates the absence of any firsthand knowledge of the problems involved.

Dangerous

What is alarming is that the Government, containing no scientists, is likely to value his pronouncements in scientific fields where his lack of training and knowledge render them worthless.

Most physicists directly concerned with nuclear research are only too anxious to learn from the biologist the possible effects of radioactivity, but there is a clear threat that the Government's policy in respect of weapons will be influenced in the main by engineers and physicists whose main interest is the verification of calculations and whose understanding of and respect for biology is negligible.

Lord Cherwell appears to have made himself the spokesman of these dangerous individuals.

Embarrassment

Pleasantries about luminous watches may entertain the students of Christ Church (where talent in biological science is not conspicuous), but they are out of place in a serious discussion of nuclear warfare.

The public will prefer to listen to biologists whose scientific objectivity is above question, rather than Lord Cherwell, who beside his scientific limitations, offers the House of Lords an admixture of technicalities and political prejudice.

Even in his own field, confidence in the

● ON BACK PAGE

The Australian Labour Party has recently expressed its belief that the present policies of the French Government in Algeria, the USSR Government in Hungary and the British Government in Cyprus are contrary to the principles of the United Nations Charter, and that self-determination for peoples capable of self-government is their right. It welcomes in contrast the creation of the new Dominion of Ghana.

Photo: KARSH of Ottawa.
Commander Sir Stephen King-Hall

H-tests: "the public can stop this immorality"
—MRS SHEILA JONES

THERE is still some time left before the word is given for the first British H-bomb test to take place.

The public can stop this immorality. There IS something we can do. It has to be done NOW.

This is the message of Mrs. Sheila Jones, Secretary of the National Council for the Abolition of Nuclear Weapon Tests*, whom I interviewed on Monday.

Just as a strong show of public disapproval with the Government's policy over Suez was instrumental in stopping war there, so would sufficient public opinion against the tests succeed in preventing them, believes Mrs. Jones.

*29 Gt. James St., London, W.C.1.

"I think there is still a chance that the British Government will abandon the tests," she told Peace News on Monday.

"People can use the new film, 'Shadow of Hiroshima.' That is a good beginning and can be followed up by protest meetings, letters to local and the national Press, to the Prime Minister and MPs—and to wives of MPs.

"There are several petitions. We do not have one of our own, but our ideas are

By Mavis James

similar to those expressed in the petition drawn up by the Fellowship Party. The Liberal Party is also running a petition.

☐ ON BACK PAGE

On the plinth of Nelson's Column in Trafalgar Square last Sunday at the Stop the H-test meeting : Dr. Edith Summerskill, Mrs. L. John Collins (standing), Vera Brittain (seated), Shiela Steele at microphone and Mrs. Shiela Jones (standing).
More pictures and report on page 6.

HAROLD STEELE OFF AGAIN TODAY

HAROLD STEELE is expected to leave New Delhi today, Friday, for either Tokio or Fiji en route to the Pacific H-test area.

The Emergency Committee for Direct Action against Nuclear War, with £5,000 available, are endeavouring to contact boats staying in the H-test area.

Mr. Steele finally received his visa for Japan on May 3 after some delay. On April 26 Acting Japanese Consul-General in London, Mr. Ryozo Sunobe, wrote to Mr. Steele that his application for a visa had "been carefully studied by the Japanese authorities concerned, and I am to state that the Japanese authorities are prepared to grant a visa only on your assurance that

★ ON BACK PAGE

Peace News, a pacifist newspaper first published in 1936, provided a vital means of communication for people in the developing anti-nuclear movement. This issue features Harold Steele's attempt to sail into the Pacific before the British H-bomb test could take place, in May 1957 (see article, bottom right). His attempt failed, but he did achieve worldwide publicity.

Local and national demonstrations against the H-bomb tests continued throughout 1957-8.

Above Church representatives join a Hackney protest led by the Mayor and councillors, June 1957.

Right In April 1954, six Labour MPs brought together a wide range of peace, church and labour organizations to form the Hydrogen Bomb National Committee. One million signatures were collected on a petition calling for a disarmament conference and the strengthening of the UN. These modest demands did not inspire a mass movement; despite a successful march *(bottom right)* and rally *(opposite)* in September 1957, the committee was wound up at the end of that year.

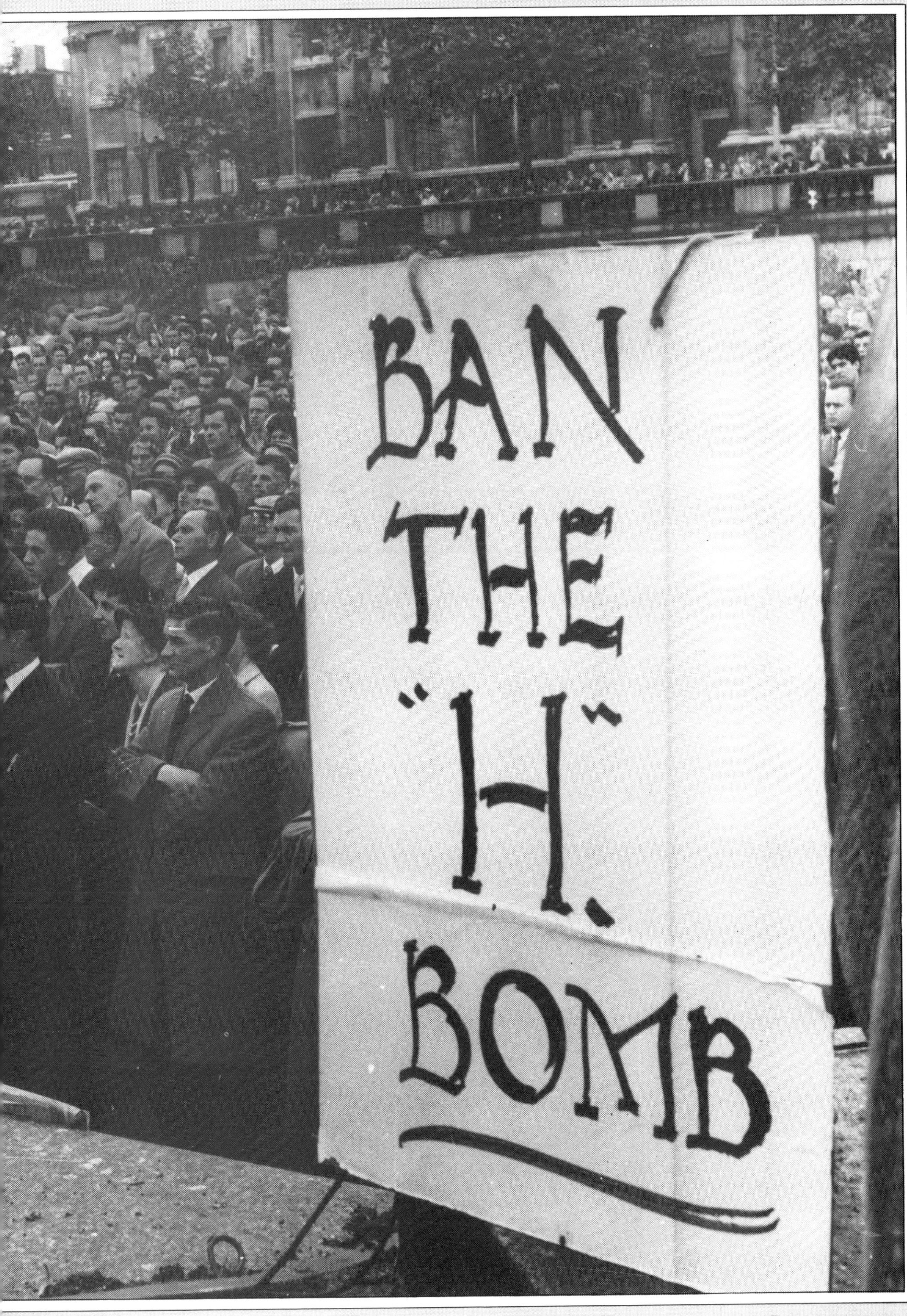
BAN
THE
"H"
BOMB

Above British Peace Committee supporters marching away from the House of Commons where they had delivered a six-point peace plan to MPs, January 1958. The image of the 'duffle-coated' peace-marcher was to be ridiculed by the popular press for the next 30 years.

Opposite Frank Cousins was a key figure in the struggle for the adoption of a policy of unilateral nuclear disarmament within the Labour movement. Speaking as General Secretary of the Transport and General Workers Union, he was at the centre of the two great Labour Party conference crises over defence policy.

In 1957 his unilateralist motion was defeated when Nye Bevan made opposition to it a test of loyalty, asserting that it would result in the Foreign Secretary 'going naked into the conference chamber'. In 1960 Cousins triumphed, causing Hugh Gaitskell, the party leader, to promise to 'fight, fight and fight again to save the party we love'.

Gaitskell succeeded in reversing the position in 1961, but Frank Cousins remained committed and his influence within the Labour movement undoubtedly contributed to the success of the unilateralists in later years.

Above J. B. Priestley and Bertrand Russell at the Central Hall inaugural meeting of CND, 17th February 1958.

Right Central Hall, Westminster (capacity 3,000) couldn't accommodate all those who wanted to hear about the new campaign. In her book *Left, Left, Left*, Peggy Duff recalled the flood of applications for sixpenny tickets, which led to her booking four additional halls for overflow meetings.

Far right This policy statement produced on the night after the launch meeting provided the basis for the future constitution of CND.

NUCLEAR DISARMAMENT

MASS MEETING
CENTRAL HALL WESTMINSTER

Michael Foot
Stephen King-Hall
J.B. Priestley
Bertrand Russell
A.J.P. Taylor
CHAIRMAN: *Canon L.John Collins*

MONDAY 17 FEBRUARY 1958

TICKETS: 6ᵈ

MARCH FROM LONDON TO ALDERMASTON

Campaign for NUCLEAR DISARMAMENT

The purpose of the Campaign is to press for a British iniative to reduce the nuclear peril and to stop the armaments race

We shall seek to persuade the British people that Britain must :

A renounce unconditionally the use or production of nuclear weapons and refuse to allow their use by others in her defence ?

B use her utmost endeavour to bring about negotiations at all levels for agreement to end the armaments race and to lead to a general disarmament convention ?

C invite the co-operation of other nations, particularly non-nuclear powers, in her renunciation of nuclear weapons.

In pressing for this unconditional renunciation by Britain the Campaign realises the need for action on particular issues, pending success in its major objectives, and we believe that Britain must :—

A halt the patrol flights of aeroplanes equipped with nuclear weapons ;

B make no further tests of nuclear weapons ;

C not proceed with the agreement for the establishment of missile bases on her territory ;

D refuse to provide nuclear weapons for any other country.

146 FLEET STREET, LONDON, E.C.4

Fleet Street 4175

Above Easter marches from Aldermaston to London became synonymous with CND, but the first march, *from* London *to* Aldermaston, in May 1958, was the idea of Hugh Brock, editor of *Peace News* and a member of the Direct Action Committee.

The Atomic Weapons Research Establishment (AWRE) at Aldermaston is the home of the British bomb. Warheads designed and built at Aldermaston are manufactured at the nearby Royal Ordnance Factory (ROF) Burghfield. Neither site appears on current Ordnance Survey maps, and ROF Burghfield is still listed as an artificial limb factory.

On the sign: UGANDA CALLS BRITAIN FOR NUCLEAR DISARMAMENT BAN H-BOMBS NO ROCKET BASES ON BRITISH SOIL.

Opposite top and bottom Students and teachers have always been active supporters, pamphlet-writers and organizers in CND. In the early days there was CUCND – Colleges and Universities CND – and later Student CND. Today Teachers for Peace exists as an autonomous organization.

Above International support and links with liberation struggles around the world feature frequently in CND's history.

Overleaf Aldermaston marchers gather in Trafalgar Square for the rally which preceded the march in 1958, and provided its climax in subsequent years.

LITTLEWOODS
FIRST STEP TO PEACE
H-BOMB
NUCLEAR DISARMAMENT
FROM FEAR
MAKE FRIENDS
BRITAIN
U.S.A. RUSSIA
BOMBS FOR
NUCLEAR

While Canon Collins and Earl Russell were probably CND's most publicly identified personalities, women were its most effective organizers.

Above Peggy Duff, seen here in what she described as 'one of those beastly, bustling slum offices', was CND's General Secretary from 1958-67, and widely acknowledged as the architect of its early successes.

In the beginning there were just three members of staff, though this increased during the peak years to over 40. But no matter how many people were employed, unpaid volunteers were always in demand, and no office ever seemed able to provide a desk or chair for everyone.

Above Pat Arrowsmith (on the right), always involved in direct action, laid particular emphasis on dialogue with workers in the defence industry, as on this nine-week picket of Aldermaston, photographed in the summer of 1958.

Right Dr Sheila Jones, herself an atomic physicist, was secretary of the National Campaign Against Atomic Weapon Tests and then a member of the CND Executive. She is seen here with her two daughters. Today she is CND's archivist.

THEY WHO WENT TO SWAFFHAM

JUST who were the people who went to prison for 14 days after the Swaffham rocket base demonstration? Peace News has set out to answer this question, and the following is the result:

First in alphabetical order is **Geoffrey Alexander** (aged 27), who likes to play the clarinet and sing madrigals, teaching the latter to his fellow detainees in the cell of the North London Police Court. Teacher, Quaker, Labour League of Youth Secretary, and member of International Voluntary Service, the pick-and-shovel peacemaking body. A founder member of the Edinburgh University Pacifist Association, he spent five weeks in Saughton Prison as a conscientious objector. While in Brixton Prison he had to battle with his asthma.

★

Pat Arrowsmith (28) is field organiser of the Direct Action Committee and had the full glare of Press publicity turned upon her. **David Bell** (24) is a member of the Pacifist Youth Action and London Anarchist Groups. An electronic engineer, he describes himself both as an agnostic and a " refugee from the Minister of Labour and National Service ": he claims unconditional exemption from military service. He did not complete his sentence at Brixton Prison owing to the death of his father. His cell was on the floor below that of **Hugh Brock** (44), editor of Peace News, whose wife and two children joined in the march of solidarity from Brixton to Holloway.

Among the Quakers in Holloway is **Joyce Brodden** (27), assistant in a public library. She took part in the Hungary-Egypt Pilgrimage as well as the Aldermaston Picket and several marches. She is a member of the National Association of Local Government Officers and the Library Association.

April Carter (21), Secretary of the Direct Action Committee, whose organising ability was revealed when she undertook responsibility for the vigil which followed the Aldermaston March, is a leading member of the British Fellowship of the Friends of Truth. Her second stay in Holloway saw her separated from **Mary Chisholm** (39), who was sent to Strangeways Prison for her sentence after being remanded to Holloway.

Mary Chisholm is a Quaker and a physiotherapist, employed at a clinic for spastic children. She is secretary of the Macclesfield CND and played a leading part in the Quaker house-to-house H-canvass covering the whole of Macclesfield (pop. 35,981). A member of the Cheshire Quakers Monthly Meeting Peace Committee, Friends Vegetarian Society, and of the Chartered Society of Physiotherapy.

★

Philip Cook (22), who fasted in Norwich Prison, is an atheist-socialist member of the Communist Party. He served 93 days in prison after becoming a CO while serving in the RAF. An ex-railway clerk of no present occupation, he took part in the Aldermaston March, and is a member of the Pacifist Youth Action Group. The actual obstruction of work at Pickenham was the most important thing for him.

The only value in the " witness " element and in the press coverage, he says, was the possibility of increased recruitment of obstructors.

" I do not believe that these weapons will be abolished by any other means. The people of this country are completely without conscience in this field."

Mrs. Liesel Dales (42), Gillingham, Kent, housewife with three daughters, aged 18, 12 and 11, and a former Roman Catholic, was imprisoned in Austria in the '30s for her activities against Nazism. Is a determined opponent of all forms of totalitarianism. A member of the Business and Professional Women's Association, she is also Secretary of the Medway Town's CND and took part in the Aldermaston picket.

A man whose name is known throughout the South Wales mining villages, **John Denaithorne** (63), is Warden of the Dowlais Educational Settlement. A sculptor, he worked with Eric Aumonier, Eric Gill and Jacob Epstein on the large carved panels high up on St. James' Park Underground Station.

He served with a Quaker relief mission in the great Russian famine of 1921-3 and gave up his work as a sculptor to work in South Wales for the Coalfields Distress Committee. Today he is Chairman of Cardiff and Region Africa Council (Africa Bureau) and of the Merthyr Board for Conscientious Objectors. He is a member of the Advisory Committee for N.E. Glamorgan of the National Assistance Board, of his area Council for Social Service, of the Race Relations Committee of the Society of Friends. We need hardly add that he is single, or that he has made three voyages round the world.

Francis Deutsch (32), solicitor's clerk of Hull, is married with a 22-month-old daughter. (" Wives and mothers waiting at home had a harder task than we jail-birds "). He took part in the first march and demonstration at the Aldermaston weapons plant when it was being built in 1952, was founder and chairman of the London School of Economics Pacifist Society, and leader and organiser of the " Coast-to-Coast " march last year. A member of the Peace Pledge Union, he believes that as the strangle-hold of the Establishment closes channels of mass communication to minorities, progressive people will have to have recourse to other methods, and that Gandhi's independence movement has shown a way both practicable and compatible with Christian and pacifist principles.

Ian Dixon (22) has a long and inspiring record of pacifist activity behind him. At one time employed at the Colonial Office, he graduated to a pacifist outlook, left the Colonial Office, and was before long secretary of the Pacifist Youth Action Group. He and David Graham hitch-hiked to India and worked with the Land Gift Movement. Has also worked hard with International Voluntary Service. He is now at Swansea University studying for a social science diploma.

Several years ago he organised a weeklong day and night picket at Wormwood Scrubs Prison and it is not surprising to find him, in his present surroundings, on the National Executive of the Combined Universities CND.

★

Frances Edwards (30), an Oxford housewife with a son of 12, took part in the Aldermaston picket and helped to organise the march to the U.S. base at Brize Norton. Because of her great abhorrence of nuclear weapons, she came to London in 1953 from Sussex to " do something about it."

" I joined the British Peace Committee as this seemed at the time the only organisation taking a positive stand against nuclear war. We made very little headway in getting support, and I think this was probably because it is essentially a Communist organisation. CND and Direct Action have enabled people to come together and voice their opinion without the fear of being labelled Communist or fellow-traveller and without having to follow the dictates of any political party.

" I can't call myself a pacifist, but I am prepared to believe that pacifism is the only answer to the situation today."

Christopher Farley (24), Quaker and journalist on Peace News staff, was in Wormwood Scrubs prison for five months in 1955 as a conscientious objector. A member of the Peace Pledge Union and on the Central Board of Conscientious Objectors, he is also a member of the National Union of Journalists.

David Graham (27), married with one child, hitch-hiked to India with Ian Dixon and walked with Vinoba Bhave in Trichinopoly, later working with International Voluntary Service at a leper colony. Has left peace slogans chalked up in the following prisons: Chelmsford, Wormwood Scrubs, Brixton, Norwich and Wandsworth.

Cyril King (50), whose home is in the Mile End district, East London, describes himself as a voluntary agitator as well as a member of the Peace Pledge Union and the Fellowship of Reconciliation.

Alan Longman (27) is a forestry research worker at present doing a Ph.D. at Manchester.

Leader of a number of Quaker work camps, he feels that " the H-bomb causes the pacifist to re-think his position as much as the non-pacifist." Finds many people interested in Swaffham and its implications and has already spoken to over 100 students following a showing of the film of the demonstration. Says his wife " is 100 per cent with me in this thing, and I am *sending* her to prison next time."

A laboratory assistant and Quaker, **Oliver Mahler** (26) is a member of Univer-

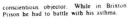

Top, left to right: Joyce Brodden, Frances Edwards, April Carter, Philip Cook (Photo: *Walthamstow Guardian*), Hugh Brock (Photo: *North London Press*). Below, left to right: Anthony Maurice-Jones, John Dennithorne, David Graham with Ian Dixon on their way to India, Liesl Dales, Francis Deutsch, and Alan Longman flirting with a mountain goat.

" This action," she told Peace News, " was made possible for me by the cheerful co-operation of my family (husband and son, aged 16) and the care and help which was freely given to them and to me by our friends."

★

sities and Left Review Club, Fellowship of Reconciliation, and the Pacifist Youth Action Group, says that though chronologically he was a pacifist first and a Christian second (" it was through pacifism I became interested in Christianity ") yet philosophically he is a Christian first and a pacifist as a consequence.

Anthony Maurice-Jones (18) risked being sent down from Cambridge after one term. " A year ago I would have scorned the Swaffham demonstration, although I would have agreed with its aims. But last year I hitch-hiked to and through India, and I became convinced of the efficacy of bashing one's head against a brick wall." An agnostic, he recognises, with Gandhi, the " God that is found in the hearts of the dumb millions."

Laurens (John) Otter (28), who also fasted in Norwich, is a school teacher at present waiting to continue studies. A member of the Common Wealth Party and the priciple pacifist organisations. He is an Anglo-Catholic.

[To be continued]

Following the launch of the Russian Sputnik in October 1957, the USA perceived a 'missile gap'. As a consequence, Britain agreed to take American intermediate-range Thor missiles. Bases in East Anglia were rapidly prepared for their deployment. The Direct Action Committee (DAC) organized its first major civil disobedience action by blockading the entrance to the construction site at RAF Swaffham in Norfolk, 1959.

THE DIRECT ACTION COMMITTEE AGAINST NUCLEAR WAR

344 SEVEN SISTERS ROAD, LONDON, N.4.

STAMFORD HILL 7062   27/10/59

COMMITTEE MEMBERS :—Pat Arrowsmith, Hugh Brock, April Carter, Frances
Edwards, Inez Randall, Michael Randle, The Rev.
Michael Scott, Allen Skinner, Will Warren.

NEW YEAR PROTEST AT HARRINGTON ROCKET BASE
(second circular)

PLEASE RAISE THIS WIT

Completed Rocket Sites

Since sending out the first circular
have found out more about what hap
built.   VIRTUALLY NO TRAFFIC A
OF THE BASE.   It would almost cer
protest which involved trying to prever
At Swaffham Last Year the rocket base
obliged constantly to go on and off t
sitting down in the entrance.

At Harrington, which is a completed
way.   We shall demonstrate that this
turned into a Thor rocket site.   We sh
uses.

THE AIM OF THE PROTEST A
ENTER THE SITE AND F

The Situation at Harrington

The actual rocket base is complete
located on an ex-airfield.   It is very c
fence along the road and the security
wire.

Above Thor missiles were also sited at RAF
Harrington, in Northamptonshire. The Direct Action
Committee members – note their names – called for an
attempt to 'reclaim' the Thor base at Harrington by
establishing a camp on the site, October 1959.

Following the Swaffham action Canon Collins issued a
statement dissociating CND from civil disobedience.
But controversy within the movement produced a
modified response, and the DAC action at Harrington
was supported by a CND march in January 1960.

Left There were Direct Action Committees outside
London, too. Here, on 30th July 1970, twenty
members of the Northern DAC demonstrate outside
the main gate at RAF Finningley, a V-bomber base in
Yorkshire. The original picture caption reads: 'Miss
Carol Taylor, Latin teacher at Urmston Grammar
School, reading a protest petition to the police'.

In October 1959 Harold Macmillan led the Tories to their third successive victory at the polls. Britain's nuclear role was increasing and CND growing spectacularly. By the end of 1959, CND had hundreds of groups and tens of thousands of supporters prepared to take a variety of actions.

Above Leaving Aldermaston for London, Easter 1960. Among others pictured are Canon John Collins, the first Chairman of CND, Jacquetta Hawkes, Professor Ritchie Calder, and the Labour MPs, Michael Foot, Barbara Castle and Frank Allaun.

Right Scottish groups, always very active in CND, never failed to make the long journey south for the four-day English march. Despite the discomfort and the logistics, they managed to bring banners too, thus advertising the nationwide support for CND.

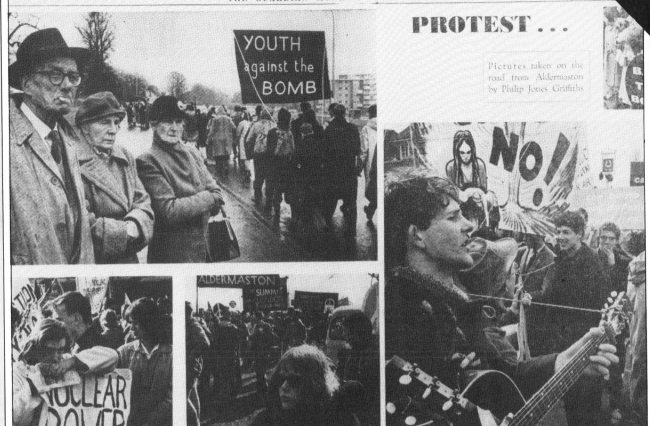

PROTEST . . .

Pictures taken on the road from Aldermaston by Philip Jones Griffiths

YOUTH against the BOMB

NO!

NUCLEAR POWER

ALDERMASTON

Above From the beginning CND's youth wing has been renowned for its enthusiasm and exuberance, and its healthy lack of respect for the 'leadership'. The music of individual players and marching bands has lifted many a flagging spirit on thousands of CND marches.

PEACE COMMITTEE OF THE SOCIETY OF FRIENDS (QUAKERS)

Quakers say NO to all WAR

Left The end of the 1960 Easter march enters Trafalgar Square in London. Quakers have probably contributed more to peace movements worldwide than any other single group.

On the eve of the Labour Party conference in October 1960, at which unilateralists were poised for success, an internal CND crisis became public. Lord Russell and Canon Collins were locked in a major row resulting from Russell's involvement in a new civil disobedience organization – the Committee of 100 (replacing DAC). Within a matter of weeks Russell had resigned as President of CND.

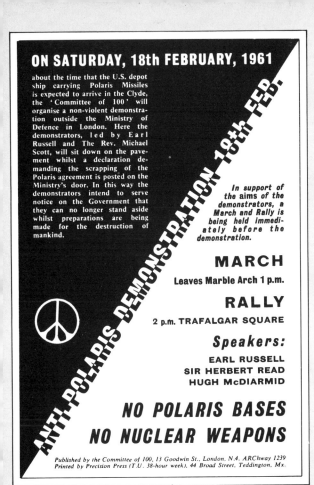

Left and opposite The Committee's first major action at the Ministry of Defence, February 1961, attracted thousands to protest against the government's decision to allow the United States to use the Holy Loch in Scotland as a base for their Polaris submarines. Surprisingly, there were no arrests. Bertrand Russell is sitting in the centre, under the banner.

Below Following the success of the February sit-down, the Committee planned a similar action for 29th April 1961. This time 826 people were arrested.

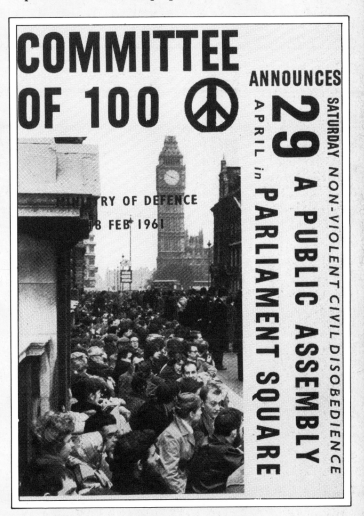

CND marchers protest in Glasgow.

Daily Mirror

3d.   Wednesday, September 13, 1961   No. 17,959

Ban-Bomb rebels refuse to 'Keep peace'

JAILED—THE STAR SIT-DOWNERS

PHILOSOPHER	AUTHORESS	PLAYWRIGHT	PARSON	SOCIAL WORKER	PLAYWRIGHT	COUNCILLOR	POET

..Seven days	..Seven days	..One month	..One month	..One month	..One month	..One month	..One month
Earl Russell	Countess Russell	Arnold Wesker	Rev. Michael Scott	Jane Noel-Buxton	Robert Bolt	Anne Kerr	Christopher Logue

Black Maria for Earl Russell

By MIRROR REPORTERS

EARL RUSSELL, the eighty-nine-year-old philosopher, was in jail last night. So were his wife, Countess Russell, and thirty other prominent members of the Committee of 100, the anti-nuclear weapons group.

All had refused to be bound over on summonses accusing them of inciting members of the public to commit a breach of the peace next Sunday.

The committee's past activities have included sit-down demonstrations in London. Next Sunday, it was alleged at Bow-street court yesterday, 10,000 demonstrators are planning to block the area round Parliament-square.

LORD RUSSELL—better known as Bertrand Russell, holder of the Order of Merit and regarded as one of the world's greatest

LADY RUSSELL GOES, TOO

1961 was a year of increasing tension with the deployment of US nuclear submarines in Scotland, French nuclear tests, and a NATO agreement that West Germany could use nuclear-powered destroyers. The Berlin Wall was built and a Soviet-initiated moratorium on weapons testing was ended by the Russians. CND organized a 'march of shame' to the Soviet embassy.

Top Opposition to American nuclear submarines continued and demonstrations were planned by the Committee of 100. As a result, more than half the Committee were arrested and required to be 'bound over'. Thirty-two people refused and were jailed.

Left The demonstrations went ahead as planned despite a ban under the Public Order Act on Trafalgar Square. 351 people were arrested at the Holy Loch demonstration shown here; 1,314 in Trafalgar Square.

31

The first phase of CND activity peaked in 1962. The Aldermaston march that year was the biggest ever, with more than 100,000 people at the rally.

Above A silent vigil was held at the Assembly in Edinburgh.

Left Attention focused, too, on the disarmament conference in Geneva where women from ten nations went to lobby delegates, April 1962.

But the year ended with the Cuba missile crisis, and the British government's decision to buy American Polaris missiles for a new British submarine-based nuclear force.

Almost from its inception CND was involved with similar movements abroad, not least because of the international renown of some of its leading members. This resulted in CND attending international conferences in Germany, Yugoslavia and Ghana, and also hosting one in Oxford.

Above In July 1962, a broadly-based CND delegation attended the World Peace Council congress in Moscow. To the alarm of some of their colleagues, Committee of 100 members produced leaflets in Russian and 'demonstrated' in Red Square. Although their banner was seized by the authorities, the demonstrators managed to achieve some dialogue with Moscow citizens.

Right The arrival of the US Navy's newest submarine depot ship, *Huntley,* produced a new round of protest in Scotland. Here demonstrators who were keeping watch since the early hours (continually stamping their feet to keep warm) raise their placards as the ship sails into the US Polaris base at Holy Loch, 9th January 1963.

Below During the 1963 Aldermaston march, an anonymous group called 'Spies for Peace' distributed a pamphlet revealing the existence of a network of underground bunkers which would become Regional Seats of Government (RSG) after a nuclear attack. It was sensational news. Here activists who had left the Aldermaston march are seen coming out of Warren Row RSG, near Henley on Thames.

Left More direct action, this time by the London Committee of 100 at Ruislip USAF base – headquarters of the United States airforce in Britain, Easter Saturday, 1964.

Below Decline in support for CND in the mid-sixties was probably accelerated by two events – the signing of the Partial Test Ban Treaty by the UK, USA and USSR in 1963, and the growing intervention of US troops in Vietnam. By 1965, opposition to the Vietnam war was beginning to dominate CND campaigning.

This photo shows key women active in the disarmament movement throughout their lives: (from left to right) Sheila Oakes, Chairperson CND 1967-8 and General Secretary National Peace Council; Olive Gibbs, Oxford City Councillor and Chairperson CND 1964-7; and the late Peggy Duff, CND's first General Secretary.

Left and below Pre-publicity for CND's Easter march, 1965.

Opposite, top Britain's nuclear weapons were not entirely forgotten. Here CND demonstrators march outside ROF Burghfield on 6th August 1966, commemorating the bombing of Hiroshima, and questioning – yet again – the morality of nuclear weapons' manufacture.

Opposite, bottom In a daring display reminiscent of the fatal suffragette action by Emily Davidson (who threw herself under the King's horse on Derby Day, 1913), members of the Ascot Action Group of the Committee of 100 hold a banner in front of the royal procession on Ladies' Day at Ascot, 22nd June 1967.

Police use horses to try and prevent London's biggest ever anti-Vietnam demonstration from entering Grosvenor Square, opposite the American Embassy, on 18th March 1968. Violence broke out on both sides and 300 people were arrested.

STOP the war in VIETNAM

Nuclear disarmament campaigners set off from Trafalgar Square on their march to Aldermaston.

Thin march towards future

By MARTIN WOOLLACOTT

A FEW PEOPLE are still left in this country who have not learned how to live with the Bomb, and yesterday about 700 of them set off from Trafalgar Square for the Atomic Weapons Research Establishment at Aldermaston, Berkshire.

They marched behind the banner used in the first CND march in 1958.

It was a pitifully small crowd by 1963 standards, when an estimated 100,000 packed into the square for the end of that year's march. But, according to the CND general secretary, Mr Dick Nettleton, who is used to parrying questions about the decline of CND : " It means something that CND is still there, is still marching."

In any case, he argues, CND, does its work now in

quieter and more effective ways. It has, he claimed yesterday, more widespread connections now with trade unions and the Labour Party than it had in 1963, when it was at the height of its success. " In three years, we may have the Labour Party again," he said, " and this time we'll keep it."

The campaign's hope, he implied, is that nuclear weapons will once again become a live issue when the present Government, or the next, has to make a decision to replace or upgrade the present Polaris force. Either the purchase of Poseidon from the United States, or an attempt to create a European nuclear force with the French would make the bomb a central issue again. Then, it is argued, CND would be able to act effectively.

For the moment, however, the Bomb remains low on the list of protest issues—lower than pollution or the Irish Question. None of the big names turned up at the rally to start the march and only one MP was around, although it was hoped some others might join during the three-day march to Aldermaston. This year, the march is very specifically a return to CND's origins, for it is the first year since 1958 that it has gone from London to Aldermaston, instead of the other way round.

Aldermaston, Mr Nettleton told the marchers, is " still the place where they are working overtime to improve the wretched Bomb, to make it move faster, to make it kill more people."

Down in the crowd of wait-

ing marchers, Paul Haines, aged 16, from a Birmingham grammar school, stands holding a placard which reads " No European Bomb." Why has he come ? " We don't want the H-bomb," he says. Well, neither do a lot of people, but they're not here in Trafalgar Square. " We don't want the H-bomb," he repeats, with slightly more emphasis.

Gay Liberation is there, smarter than almost anybody else. " Gay Liberation isn't a narrow, chauvinistic group just for gay people—we're part of the people who want to change society as a whole," an organiser said. " Most gay people must be against the bomb : gay people know what it's like to be oppressed."

Mrs Bridget Wright, an attractive 50-year-old, says it is her eleventh year on the march. Of course, CND has declined, she says : " So many other causes have grown out of it, they have diverted energy away from it. But protest on so many issues has grown out of what we started.".

March ban may be lifted

Continued from page 1

cannon, and barbed wire " could have obvious implica-

what he meant and yesterday the Civil Rights Association, whose own march in Derry last January ended in a confronta-

rally " was without the consent of the organisers." The advertisement went on to say that Vanguard regretted that

Above Hugh Jenkins and Fenner Brockway, preparing for another CND rally, 1974. Both are lifelong activists in the disarmament movement, former Labour MPs and now active campaigners in the House of Lords. In 1980 Fenner Brockway and the late Lord Noel-Baker formed the World Disarmament Campaign.

Opposite CND returns to its roots and marches back to Aldermaston, Easter 1972.

The spread of American and Russian bases, and patrols by nuclear-armed ships, led to vociferous protests in non-nuclear countries, including Japan, Australia and New Zealand.

Here New Zealand activists sail small boats into the wake of an American nuclear-armed submarine. In 1973 New Zealand sponsored a resolution, adopted by the UN, for the South Pacific to be declared nuclear-free.

In 1984, New Zealand elected a government dedicated to non-nuclear policies, and visits by such ships were prohibited.

CND's revival as a mass movement began in Scotland where, throughout the 1970s, demonstrations were mounted against both American and British Polaris submarines.

Above The head of the Faslane march, 1975.

Opposite top The peace cruise at Holy Loch, 1977.

Opposite bottom Buddhist monks with Bruce Kent, then Chairperson and subsequently General Secretary of CND, at Faslane.

Opposition to nuclear power grew worldwide in the 1970s, and successive annual conferences of CND adopted motions recognizing the link between civil and military nuclear energy, and committing the movement to campaign against both.

Right Friends of the Earth demonstration outside the Atomic Energy Research establishment at Lucas Heights in Sydney, Australia, 16th January 1977.

Below Protests against the building of a new nuclear waste reprocessing plant at Windscale (now called Sellafield), 29th April 1978.
   The plant was designed to handle not only British nuclear waste from civil and military reactors, but waste from other countries as well. Plutonium recovered from nuclear waste is an essential component of nuclear warheads.

Left On 28th March 1979, a nuclear power plant at Three Mile Island, Harrisburg, USA, suffered the worst accident then known in the history of nuclear technology. The young woman whose T-shirt boasts 'I survived Three Mile Island' could suffer later in life. A significant amount of radiation escaped into the atmosphere and is expected to cause human cancers within twenty years.

Right In Britain details of minor leaks and accidents were constantly being made public by anti-nuclear groups – as was the transportation of nuclear waste through urban areas. Here women protest against the use of a North London rail line, June 1979.

Below A demonstration against prospecting for uranium (the raw material for both civil and military nuclear cycles) in County Donegal, Eire, March 1980.

THE REVIVAL

CND revived because people joined. Outrage at the secret NATO decision, revealed in December 1979, to deploy American cruise missiles in Britain, coming only seven months after a general election devoid of debate on defence, led to the formation of dozens of new anti-missile groups.

Some of the founding members were Quakers, with a long tradition of peace campaigning, some were CND members, or both, but much of the dynamism came from people who were new to the peace movement. Initially there was no certainty that CND would be the beneficiary of this upsurge, but the organization's willingness to help local groups, regardless of allegiance, gained the respect of the new activists.

Before long, most of the local groups affiliated to CND, and many individuals who were not active locally decided to show support by joining the national campaign. In 1980 both the numbers of CND groups and the national individual membership doubled, heralding a spectacular period of growth.

National and international politics provided the stimuli for ever-increasing waves of protest. The fact that NATO deployment of new American missiles affected West Germany, Holland, Belgium and Italy, as well as Britain, resulted in parallel responses and interest in European-wide co-operation.

A number of people with past roots in CND and good European contacts, notably Edward Thompson and Ken Coates (of the Bertrand Russell Peace Foundation), decided that an international threat required an international response. European Nuclear Disarmament (END), a campaign for the removal of all nuclear weapons from both East and West, was founded in February 1980. The END Appeal was sent all over Europe and formally launched, with thousands of signatures, at the end of April 1980.

Unlike CND, END did not seek to become a mass-membership organization, but more a campaign to stimulate ideas and encourage international co-operation. In July 1982, the first of the now annual conventions of European supporters of nuclear disarmament was convened by the Russell Peace Foundation with support from END.

In Britain, the announcement (on 12th December 1979) of the deployment of 160 American cruise missiles was followed by further revelations of secret decision-taking. In a parliamentary debate on defence, in January 1980, it emerged that successive governments had secretly spent £1,000m on the Chevaline programme for modernizing the Polaris fleet. Since Labour, during this period, had been elected on a commitment to run down Polaris, accountability for nuclear policy became a major debating point.

There had been secrecy, too, in civil defence planning. In February 1980, the BBC's *Panorama* programme revealed the existence of the government's pre-recorded *Protect and Survive* films, to be transmitted in the run-up to a nuclear war. The government responded by putting on sale a public information booklet of the same name.

The ridicule that followed did much to boost CND's membership but nothing to deter the government, which went on issuing circulars to public authorities and allocating more and more money to 'home defence'. Journalists such as Duncan Campbell *(New Statesman)* researched and exposed many of the deadly secrets of the nuclear state, not least government plans to intern dissenters should a nuclear war seem likely, and to carry out executions to maintain law and order after the bombs had fallen.

By mid-1980 the British government had announced the cruise deployment sites – RAF Greenham Common in Berkshire, and RAF Molesworth in Cambridgeshire – together with its intention to replace Polaris with the American Trident submarine-based missile system. The cost of the latter was estimated at over £5,000m – an estimate which subsequently doubled, resulting in substantial cuts in the conventional defence budget.

Local and regional actions multiplied, pamphlets were written, books started and key individuals began to organize support in the professions, the church, the political parties and the trade unions. In August 1980, the thirty-fifth anniversary of the atomic bombing of Japan was marked all over Britain, as a new generation discovered the grim history of nuclear warfare.

In October CND called its first major demonstration for many years – Trafalgar Square was packed as 80,000 people heard Edward Thompson urge 'feel your strength'. Local authorities recognized theirs when Manchester City Council declared itself a nuclear-free zone, and invited others to follow in a public information campaign which significantly advanced the debate.

As 1980 came to a close, Margaret Thatcher's government in Britain and Ronald Reagan's administration in the United States were firmly set on a course of massive nuclear rearmament. In the Soviet Union, an ageing Brezhnev was destined to spend his last two years increasingly embroiled in the civil war in Afghanistan.

The peace movement, however, was bursting with vitality, and several years of unprecedented growth lay ahead. In 1981 CND enlarged its national council to give due weight to regional representation, elected a new team of officers and doubled its staff. Parallel developments occurred all over Western Europe and in the United States. In the countries of the Warsaw Pact, official peace committees continued to support their government's position, while dissident voices took up some of the demands of the West and created their own peace agendas.

In the summer of 1981, a group of women in Wales took up an idea put forward by Ann Pettit, and organized a march from Cardiff to Greenham Common. Frustrated because of the lack of serious attention given to their demands *en route*, they declared that they would stay until the government agreed to a public debate on the cruise missiles.

Thus began the Greenham Women's Peace Camp, which was to inspire people throughout the world, and put the influence of feminists at the heart of the British peace movement. Local CND groups had been closely involved with the planning of the march, and such now was the changed nature of CND that support for an autonomous women's organization and for non-violent direct action became the policy of the whole movement.

NATO missile plan will go ahead

From David Fairhall
in Brussels

NATO is to press ahead with its controversial £2.5 billion plan to install a new generation of long-range nuclear missiles in Europe. The decision has been made despite Holland's refusal to have them based on its territory until the Soviet response to a parallel arms control initiative can be assessed, and in defiance of protests from the Russians.

At yesterday's meeting in Brussels, attended by defence and foreign ministers, the Dutch were joined by the Belgians and Danes in proposing either a delay, or at least that the missiles' deployment should be conditional on the Soviet Union's attitude.

These reservations were submerged, however, in a compromise which ensures that at least the 476 ground-launched Cruise missiles and Pershing II ballistic missiles planned for deployment in Britain, West Germany, and Italy, will be produced and deployed, with the possibility that a further 96 will later be based in Holland and Belgium.

Ministers also agreed at yesterday's meeting that negotiations towards a mutual reduction of nuclear weapons in Europe should begin with the Soviet Union as soon as possible.

The US Secretary of State, Mr Vance, said later that preliminary discussions with the Russians might start within the next few months, and that it had been agreed they could best be held as part of the next round of Strategic Arms Limitation Talks between the United States and the USSR—SALT III. A special consultative body has been set up by NATO to support these negotiations.

It was also agreed yesterday, according to the NATO Secretary General, Dr Joseph Luns, that " as an integral part " of the nuclear modernisation programme, 1,000 American nuclear warheads will be with-

US increase defence budget : Moscow ready for arms curb talks, both page 4

drawn from Europe as soon as possible, and that the new weapons will be counted within that reduced level.

Holland has agreed to contribute towards the £250 million cost of the new missiles' military infrastructure — which allows NATO to present yesterday's decision as unanimous.

But Holland's continued doubts about the modernisation plan were spelt out in a statement by Mr Willem Scholten, the Dutch defence minister, who said : " The Netherlands agrees that there is a need for a political and military answer to threatening developments in relation to Soviet long range theatre nuclear forces, particularly the SS 20 missile and the Backfire bomber.

" In view of the importance we attach to arms control and to the zero option as the ultimate objective in this field, the Netherlands cannot yet commit herself to the stationing of ground-launched Cruise missiles on her territory.

" The Netherlands will take a decision in December, 1981, in consultation with the Allies, on the basis of the criterion wheth-

Turn to back page, col. 2

Above The decision to deploy cruise and Pershing missiles in Europe (a decision kept secret from the British parliament) was announced on 12th December 1979. It was the signal for an unprecedented growth of anti-nuclear activity worldwide.

Two weeks later the Soviet Union invaded Afghanistan, and US President-elect Ronald Reagan signalled an end to détente by refusing to ratify the SALT II treaty.

Right 1980 witnessed the first major parliamentary debate on nuclear policy in Britain for 14 years, during which it was revealed that the previous Labour government had secretly spent £1bn updating Polaris. Changed attitudes, however, resulted in the Labour Party organizing the first national demonstration against cruise missiles, June 1980.

The Labour Party March and Rally
NUCLEAR ARMS NO PEACE YES
Assemble 12 noon Belvedere Road South Bank
Rally 3 p.m. Hyde Park
Sunday 22 June

Above END's banner on display at the Labour Party's June demonstration. Devised primarily by the writer and historian Edward Thompson, and by Ken Coates, of the Bertrand Russell Peace Foundation, European Nuclear Disarmament was a response to the dominant influence of both the USA and USSR in Europe. The END appeal was addressed to Europeans of both East and West.

Right Edward Thompson, whose other major contribution at this time was the pamphlet *Protest and Survive* – a response to the government's civil defence publication *Protect and Survive*. Both documents recruited thousands of people to END and CND.

Above Local and regional campaigns against the missiles, notably 'East Anglia against the Missiles', 'Campaign Atom' (Oxford) and the Berkshire Anti-Nuclear Campaign (BANC) sprang up in areas with existing US bases and nuclear facilities, and attracted wide public support.

On 17th June 1980, the government announced that the first cruise missile base in Britain would be RAF Greenham Common, near Newbury in Berkshire. That same evening Joan Ruddock and Geoff Peppiatt (at the head of the march, in a T-shirt) set up the Newbury Campaign Against Cruise Missiles.

Right 26th October 1980. CND called its first national demonstration for many years. Of the 80,000 attending, many were new to the movement, while others like James Cameron (seen here with his wife Moni) had never left it.

Joan Ruddock speaking at the rally in Trafalgar Square. The cruise missiles' brochure had been issued to local residents to explain the government's position. It contained the chilling sentence: 'The aim of using the missiles would be to persuade the Russian leadership, even at the eleventh hour, to draw back'.

Above On 5th November 1980, Manchester City Council declared itself a nuclear-free zone and invited other local authorities to do likewise.

Above right An anti-nuclear advertising campaign.

Right A nuclear-free council sign in Hackney, east London.

Below More anti-nuclear promotional material.

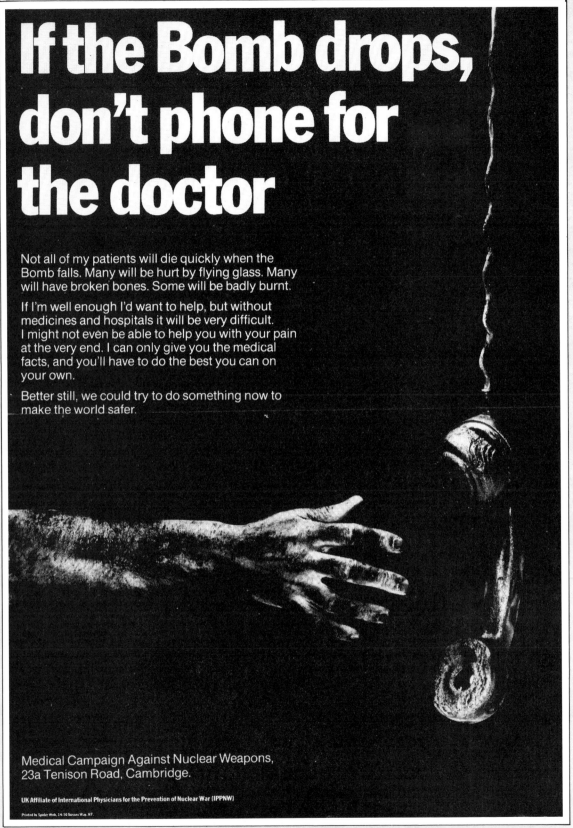

If the Bomb drops, don't phone for the doctor

Not all of my patients will die quickly when the Bomb falls. Many will be hurt by flying glass. Many will have broken bones. Some will be badly burnt.

If I'm well enough I'd want to help, but without medicines and hospitals it will be very difficult. I might not even be able to help you with your pain at the very end. I can only give you the medical facts, and you'll have to do the best you can on your own.

Better still, we could try to do something now to make the world safer.

Medical Campaign Against Nuclear Weapons, 23a Tenison Road, Cambridge.

UK Affiliate of International Physicians for the Prevention of Nuclear War (IPPNW)

Printed by Spider Web. 14-18 Sussex Way. N7.

In 1980 a group of doctors (still an influential profession) got together to form the Medical Campaign Against Nuclear Weapons. The campaign is affiliated to the International Physicians for the Prevention of Nuclear War, whose American and Soviet presidents were awarded the Nobel Peace Prize in 1986.

In 1983 The British Medical Association's Board of Science and Education published a report entitled *The Medical Effects of Nuclear Weapons* which concluded: 'The NHS could not deal with the casualties that might be expected following the detonation of a single one-megaton weapon over the UK'.

Right Non-violent direct action successfully taken by local people, who occupied a site being investigated for the possible construction of a nuclear power station at Luxullyan in the West Country.

Below In the summer of 1981 a group of women from Wales marched to Greenham Common. On arrival they requested a debate with the Minister for Defence. When their request was ignored, the women elected to stay at the base, and so the Greenham Common Peace Camp (initially with men and women) began on 5th September 1981.

Opposite Protests against the deployment of American Cruise and Pershing II missiles occurred throughout Europe, and this photo shows part of the huge march organized by CND in London, October 1981.

In addition to peace groups from all over Britain, the demonstration was supported by political parties, trade unions, and a number of specialist autonomous groups. In the foreground are the placards of BAND (Book Action for Nuclear Disarmament) and in the background, with an equally famous following, MEND (Members of Equity for Nuclear Disarmament).

Left Dutch soldiers, enjoying a political freedom unknown in most other countries, join the anti-cruise demonstration in Amsterdam, November 1981.

Below A quarter of a million Germans demonstrate in Bonn, October 1981.

In Japan there were protests, too, at the visit of
American ships carrying nuclear weapons.

Datganiad CLWYD

Chwefror 23·1982 February

the CLWYD Declaration

Mae'r penderfyniad a wnaed heddiw gan Gyngor Clwyd yn datgan eu bod yn cyhoeddi eu sir yn ddi-niwcliar, o arwyddocâd arbennig i Gymru gyfan. Yn ystod y flwyddyn a aeth heibio gwnaed penderfyniadau tebyg gan un Sir Gymreig ar ôl y llall, gan ddechrau gyda Dyfed a diweddu gyda Chlwyd.

Mae hi wedi bod yn amlwg ers tro fod pobl Cymru yn gytûn ar y mater yma. Mae'r grwpiau gwrth-niwcliar gwirfoddol sydd wedi'u ffurfio yma a thraw wedi cydweithio er mwyn ceisio cael Cymru i'w chyhoeddi ei hun yn wlad ddi-niwcliar, ac mae'r naill arolwg a deiseb ar ôl y llall wedi dangos bod cefnogaeth lethol i'r ymgyrchu ymysg pobl sy'n pryderu ynglŷn â helaethu'r haglen niwcliar ac sy'n ceisio'r hawl i leisio'u barn eu hunain am ddyfodol y ddynoliaeth.

Yn dilyn y penderfyniad yma heddiw, rydym yn gallu datgan i'r byd fod Cymru gyfan, drwy ei chynrychiolwyr etholedig democrataidd, wedi'i chyhoeddi ei hun yn wlad ddi-niwcliar. Trwy'r weithred hon mae Cymru wedi rhoi arweiniad moesol i wledydd eraill Ewrop a'r byd.

Wrth gyflwyno iddynt ein neges o obaith ac ysbrydoliaeth, rydym yn galw ar genhedloedd eraill Ewrop i roi gwybod i'r byd gymaint yw eu pryder am ddyfodol gwareiddiad. Rydym yn galw arnynt i ymdynghedu i achub Ewrop rhag dinistr llwyr drwy gymryd y cam cyntaf a chyhoeddi eu gwledydd yn ddi-niwcliar.

The decision made today by the Clwyd Council to declare its county a nuclear free zone is of special significance to the whole of Wales. During the past year similar decisions have been made by one Welsh County after another, beginning with Dyfed and culminating this very day with Clwyd.

The consensus of opinion of the Welsh people in this matter has long been evident. Local anti-nuclear groups which sprang up voluntarily have been able to co-ordinate their activities so that Wales as an entity be made a nuclear free zone, & surveys and petitions have shown the overwhelming support for their campaign by a populace which is deeply concerned by nuclear escalation and which wants the right to have its say in the future of humanity.

Because of today's decision we are now in a position to proclaim to the world that the whole of Wales, through its democratically elected representatives, has declared itself a nuclear free zone. By this action Wales has given a moral lead to the other countries of Europe and the world.

In passing on to them our message of hope and inspiration, we call upon the other nations of Europe to make known their deep concern for the future of civilization. We call upon them to commit themselves to the cause of redeeming Europe from total destruction by taking the initial step of declaring their homelands nuclear free zones

Vigorous campaigning by CND Cymru and the Welsh Anti-Nuclear Alliance converted each county in turn into a nuclear-free zone, culminating in this declaration, in February 1982, of a nuclear-free Wales.

Top and opposite Six months after its inception, the Greenham Women's Peace Camp had become a large settlement of caravans and portacabins with a communal meeting area, supported by CND and women's groups nationwide.

Above The Greenham Camp inspired many others both in Britain and overseas. Here activists set up a camp at the US forward-operating base at Fairford in Gloucestershire, February 1982.

Above Union organizers talk to construction workers at the Greenham Common site. The site was officially 'blacked', but lucrative contracts attracted many local and national firms. Peaceful picketing was undertaken by both union members and Greenham women.

Right Fran De'Ath, in the foreground, daily invited workers going to the site to stop for 'tea and a chat'. Behind her are two other founder members of the camp, Lynne Jones and Helen John.

Peace camp appeal for food

PEACE campaigners outside the US Army base at Caerwent are hoping they can cook up some more support.

The CND activists have appealed for donations of food so they can make a permanent stay outside the base.

Plaid Cymru supporters have already come to their aid and have asked people to donate tinned and packet foods to party members for the camp.

But they urge the general public to stay away from the camp, rather than turn up with food on the spot.

They fear that the public could cause an obstruction,

Top In apparent defiance of its nuclear-free status, Mid-Glamorgan County Council began to build a nuclear bunker. CND protesters took enormous risks, lying on top of its high walls while workmen continued to pour in concrete. The action, which received massive trade union and local support, was finally successful and the bunker abandoned, March 1982.

Above In numerous actions local groups all over Britain highlighted the presence of US bases in their midst. These protesters are outside the US base at Caerwent in South Wales, where nuclear warheads are stored.

The United Nations planned its second Special Session on Disarmament for the summer of 1982. In member countries throughout the world, supportive activities were planned in the hope that international relations could be improved. CND called a mass demonstration for 6th June, never suspecting that Britain would, by then, be at war with Argentina.

In the event a quarter of a million people demonstrated in London, Joan Ruddock addressed the General Assembly of the UN, and Bruce Kent spoke at the 800,000-strong demonstration organized by the US peace movement. Only five people withdrew from their membership of CND because of the movement's opposition to the Falklands war.

Above Scientists on the march, 6th June 1982. SANA is one of dozens of autonomous professional groups working for disarmament. Professor Tom Kibble of Imperial College, London, a prominent theoretical physicist, can be seen on the far left.

Opposite, top New York. The United States' largest ever peace demonstration brought to the streets an enormous variety of colour, sound and symbolism, 12th June 1982.

Right In Moscow, too, they demonstrated – though, in contrast to Western peace movements, the Soviet Peace Committee supports official government policy. Some of the banners say 'For a nuclear-free Europe'.

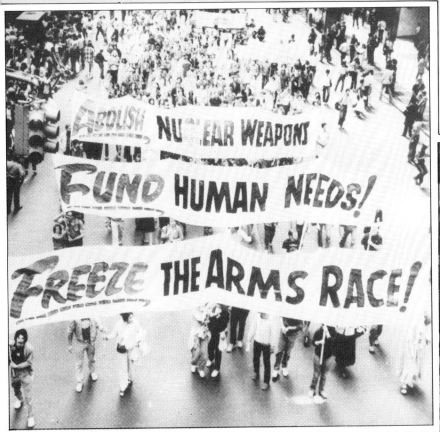

Despite the fact that growing numbers of local authorities were declaring themselves nuclear-free, the Home Office went ahead with its civil defence plans. But so many councils refused to take part in the biggest ever civil defence exercise, Hard Rock, that the government was forced to cancel it.

Opposite, top West Midlands CND demonstrating outside a civil defence conference at Moseley, 7th October. Jasper Carrott, the popular 'alternative' comedian, frequently debunked civil defence on TV.

Opposite, bottom Members of Leicester CND being shown around their local emergency control centre, following a city council decision to open the bunkers to the public. Many authorities did likewise, and many bunkers turned out to be 'leaky', ill-equipped buildings.

Above Youth CND organize an imaginative demonstration showing expected casualties in the event of a nuclear attack on the Northwood base in Hertfordshire, 4th July 1982.

Left 'Babies Against the Bomb', seen here in a lobby at Downing Street, was one of many autonomous peace groups active during this period. Involving young children in demonstrations brought attacks from right-wing journalists and politicans. The mothers countered that it was the children's future that was at stake, and their love for the children which made them act.

Below Essex groups demonstrate against the building of a nuclear bunker for councillors, April 1982.

European nuclear strategy within NATO required the building of new wartime headquarters. The location chosen in Britain was part of the Bradenham estate, owned by the National Trust. Strenuous efforts by peace campaigners and conservationists failed to frustrate the plan and the Ministry of Defence acquired the land *(above)*.

Right Part of the Bradenham estate, autumn 1982.

Above To mark the third anniversary of the NATO decision to deploy cruise missiles, 30,000 women from peace groups all over Britain (and abroad) embrace the Greenham base.

Left Personal items are left on the fence, to contrast the paraphernalia of everyday life with the planned deployment of weapons of mass destruction.

Opposite, top Members of the Upper Heyford peace camp prepare extra shelter to accommodate people joining their end-of-year blockade of the base.

Opposite, centre As construction of the silos progressed at Greenham, new and better fences were erected. The women, however, always managed to scale them.

Right At dawn on New Year's Day 1983, Greenham women dance on the half-built silos. Forty-four women were charged with breach of the peace – but the picture went round the world.

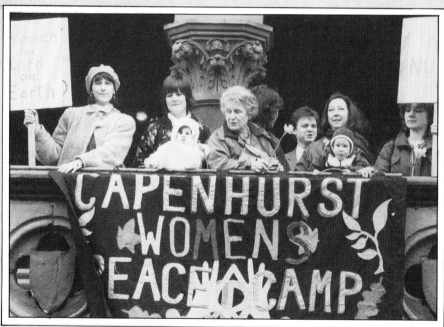

Women began to take action to draw attention to all aspects of the nuclear cycle, including the massive allocation of financial resources.

Top 'Did you order this, Sir?' – Women's International Day protest at the Bank of England, 8th March 1983.

Above Picket of Chester Court, where women were being tried following actions at the Capenhurst uranium-enrichment plant, 16th March 1983.

Villages in CND siege

By STEWART PAYNE

RESIDENTS of two villages were putting up the barricades last night ready for an Easter invasion by anti-nuclear protesters.

More than 40,000 Campaign for Nuclear Disarmament supporters are expected to descend on Burghfield Common and Greenham Common, 14 miles apart in Berkshire, for a massive demonstration.

Their plan is to blockade the Royal Ordnance Factory at Burghfield, near Reading, where nuclear

Reagan's missile plan—Page 4

warheads are made, and the Greenham Common air base, where Cruise missiles are to be sited

At midday tomorrow the protesters plan to form a human chain between the two installations, passing the Atomic Weapons Establishment at Aldermaston at the midway point.

Last night, as the demonstrators began arriving by coach, car and foot, residents unhappy about being forced to play host were making their own defence plans.

Signposts to the two establishments have been removed or blacked

Turn to Page 2, Col 2

Burghfield Stores,
Sunnyside,
Reading Road,
Burghfield Common,
Berkshire

3rd April 1983

The Editor,
Sunday Telegraph,
135 Fleet Street,
London EC4

Dear Sir,

As a grocer living in Burghfield Common fronting onto the road lined by CND last Good Friday, I feel compelled to state your article last Sunday commenting on the rubbish left behind is totally untrue.

In actual fact, Burghfield Common has not been as clean and tidy in the 11 months I have lived here as it was on the morning after the demonstration.

Customers coming into the shop on Saturday morning, a great many of whom were very anti and hostile earlier in the week, said that in all fairness to CND, they had to be congratulated, first on the behaviour of their people and secondly for the tremendous effort thad had obviously been put in to cleaning up the route. It was just impossible to believe that so many thousands had been there only the day before. On my way to Church this morning, it was apparent that not just Burghfield Common was cleared up. All the way to R.O.F. Burghfield was the same.

A Thames Valley Police Officer epitomised the spirit of the day, when late on Friday afternoon, wearing a daffodil given to him by CND, he came into the shop, his face wreathed in a smile, and said what a good day it had been and he would have CND anytime rather than a football crowd, 'You know they're for peace – they won't throw things at you'.

One final comment on litter, on Saturday afternoon I spotted 2 people with bin liners walking along each side of Reading Road. They were CND supporters, but their sacks were almost empty. Their colleagues had been there before them.

Yours faithfully,

E. Solomon.

E.M. SOLOMON

cc: C.N.D.,
11 Goodwin Street,
London N4 3HQ

In early 1983 CND began to mobilize for its most ambitious demonstration to date, a 14-mile human chain linking ROF Burghfield, AWRE Aldermaston and RAF Greenham Common. Local hysteria was whipped up by the media *(top left).*

Above The reality was somewhat different.

Left An estimated 100,000 people covered the 14-mile route in a wholly peaceful protest, 1st April 1983.

83

HESELTINE 'EXPOSES' CND LEFT

Tories briefed for poll battle

By JAMES WIGHTMAN Political Correspondent

MR HESELTINE, Defence Secretary, has written to all Conservative candidates in marginal constituencies giving them advice on how to respond to the Campaign for Nuclear Disarmament during the General Election campaign.

He has also given biographical details of leading CND personalities, drawing attention to some links with the Labour and Communist parties.

His letter was described last night by Mrs Joan Ruddock, CND's chairman, as "another example of the Government's smear campaign against the peace movement."

Mr Heseltine tells the candidates that he is writing to them because of the official policy of CND to oppose them during the election campaign.

"I think you should welcome this because the announcement has revealed the true nature and purpose of CND," he writes. The letter goes on:

By their own act they have clearly revealed what up to now has always been for some a matter of doubt.

They are an organisation led and dominated by Left-wing activists ranging through the Labour Party to the Communist Party.

Many people attracted to the peace movement will just not want to believe that behind the carefully-tuned phrases about peace lies the calculating political professionalism of full time Socialists and Communists.

'Left majority'

Mr Heseltine's letter says a clear majority of the elected members of the National Council of CND, including officers, were of the Left or extreme Left.

He adds: "And as we know, when the Left takes control in its modern manifestation it is adept at the conspiracy of control.

"All over this country we must now recognise that we face hard-line Left professionals deeply entrenched in the Labour party and the front organisations surrounding it.

"They use the arguments for peace for party political purposes.

"It is important that the public is aware of this as the defence issues are rightly debated."

Leaders listed

Giving the Tory candidates biographical details of leading CND personalities, Mr Heseltine's letter lists:

CHAIRPERSON: Joan Ruddock, Labour Parliamentary candidate 1979;

VICE-CHAIRPERSONS: Michael Pentz, Communist party candidate in the local government election, 1950s; Roger Spiller, associated with the International Socialists.

TREASURER: Mick Elliott, executive committee member of Sheffield district Labour party.

ELECTED MEMBERS OF THE NATIONAL COUNCIL: E. P. Thompson, Marxist historian, resigned from Communist party in 1956; Pat Arrowsmith, Labour party; John Cox, Communist for many years; Phil Bolsover, "member of Communist party prior to 1956; Candy Atherton, Labour party; Joy Hurcombe, secretary of Labour CND; Alisdair Beal, Labour party; Ian Davison, Communist party; Penny Auty, Labour party; Helen John, who has written in a CND conference newsletter: "There will be a great need for people to break the law. Women will not be silenced by the law of England."

'Clear majority'

Mr Heseltine added, "These 14 people constitute a clear majority of the total members of the National Council of CND including officers, elected last November, who number 26.

"In addition, three people who failed to get elected to the National Council in 1982 are now regional delegates of CND."

He listed those three as Bill Howard, who he said declared himself a Communist at the 1981 conference and was appointed CND's main fundraising co-ordinator in 1983, Sue Duerdoth, Communist; and Ron McIlroy, Communist, formerly Labour party.

He said a fourth person who failed to get elected last year but had now become a member

Continued on Back P, Col 6

Continued from Page One

CND 'EXPOSURE'

By JAMES WIGHTMAN

Continued from Page One

of the National Council was Jon Blomfield, member of the Communist party's National Peace Committee.

Mr Heseltine added: "There is at present insufficient information about the political affiliations of the remainder of the 26 elected in November last year except that there was one Liberal."

Mr Heseltine describes the sort of arguments the CND will use against the Government and says that to suggest a monopoly of concern for peace for the Labour party at the expense of the Conservatives was to disregard the irrefutable evidence of 40 years and to insult the intelligence of the British people.

He adds: "There has, therefore, to be a purpose for so preposterous a claim which is nothing to do with peace at all. And there is.

"That purpose is the advance of the Socialist and Communist cause. At its most extreme it is to argue the cause of the Soviet Union at the expense of the free societies of the West."

Mr Heseltine will extend his attack on CND when he addresses Conservatives in Exeter this afternoon.

The Prime Minister gave the defence portfolio to Mr Heseltine earlier this year because she wanted someone who she felt could effectively counter CND and Labour with its unilateral disarmament policy.

'Another smear'

Mrs Joan Ruddock, chairman of CND, said last night that Mr Heseltine's letter was another example of the "Government's smear campaign" against the peace movement.

As all the opposition parties had disarmament policies, while the Conservatives had a "rearmament" policy, it was the Government themselves who had isolated themselves from the voters," she said.

Mrs Ruddock, in Newcastle for a local television debate, added: "It is an attempt to suggest that there is something underhand about our campaign. Nothing could be further from the truth.

"This is a democratic and open campaign. Candidates in our elections all have to give their biographies, including their political affiliations, and members then have a secret ballot. Nothing could be more open."

Mrs Ruddock also denounced Mr Heseltine's allegation that the leaders of CND were full-time Socialists.

"What is that? I think the recent debate about my position with the Citizens' Advice Bureau has proved that in fact we are all doing this in our spare time and are not drawing salaries."

"To suggest that CND is campaigning for anything other than disarmament is simply fallacious," she said.

CND's leading lady in clash over cash cut

by Martin Kettle

THE GOVERNMENT is cutting back its grant to citizens' advice bureaus partly because of displeasure at the political activities of the chairman of the Campaign for Nuclear Disarmament, Joan Ruddock, who is a bureau employee in Reading.

The cut has been personally authorised by Dr Gerard Vaughan, the junior trade minister and MP for Reading South. Vaughan wrote to the National Association of Citizens' Advice Bureaus on March 23 telling them that they will receive a grant of £3 million for the current financial year, compared with £6 million last year. Future funding will be considered in September, the minister said.

No reasons for the action were given in the letter. However, at earlier talks with CAB representatives, Dr Vaughan said there was anxiety in his constituency that Joan Ruddock was using public money given to the CAB to subsidise CND activity.

According to Lady Ricketts, the chairman of the bureaus' national association, Vaughan was unhappy with the efficiency and quality of advice given by some bureaus, as well as with "inappropriate political activity". When pressed to give examples, he cited the activities of "the organiser of the Reading bureau," Mrs Ruddock.

"We have been pressing for details on all these matters since last summer," said Lady Ricketts yesterday. "So far we have been given none. All that the minister will say is that he has had complaints and that they are not frivolous."

She said that an internal inquiry had been carried out into Mrs Ruddock's position which had concluded that she was not mixing up her bureau work with her CND activity. "Joan Ruddock is extremely well thought of in the CAB service," said Lady Ricketts. Further support for Mrs Ruddock was voiced yesterday by citizens' adv[...] in Reading a[...]

Vaughan [...] comment [...] spokesman [...] of Trade co[...] in grant to [...] made person[...] because of c[...] control was [...] over bureau [...] cause of "a[...] plaints" abo[...]

Britain's [...] bureaus hav[...] of whom [...] volunteers. [...] five million [...] public each [...] from the [...] supports the [...] offices of th[...] Local bureau [...] Reading, ar[...] national go[...] local authori[...]

Joan Rud[...] organiser of the Reading office for nearly four years. Last year, when she became chairman of CND, she was allowed to continue her job on a part-time basis.

The cut in grant was criticised by the Labour Party's trade spokesman, Peter Archer. "It's like the Queen of Hearts, Sentence first, verdict afterwards", he said yesterday. "This is an appalling way for the government to administer a service which is of fundamental importance in breaking down inequalities. If Dr Vaughan has complaints, he should come clean with The National Association of Citizens' Advice Bureau and not keep his reasons a closely guarded secret."

The national association has responded to Vaughan, saying that it is fully aware of its responsibilities as receivers of public funds and reaffirming the political impartiality of the advice service.

1983 was general election year. From the outset, there appeared to be an orchestrated media campaign against CND, its officers and General Secretary. The Secretary of State for Defence set up a propaganda unit specifically to attack CND and, as Cathy Massiter was later to reveal, sought assistance in this from MI5.

Above The Minister of Consumer Affairs, Dr Gerard Vaughan, put pressure on the Citizens' Advice Bureau service, Joan Ruddock's employers, by threatening to withhold half the national organization's annual grant, citing 'political activities' within the service. The National Association of CABs stoutly defended its record and its personnel. The resulting furore led to two parliamentary debates during which Dr Vaughan was forced to withdraw his 'implied' criticism.

Left Support for Christian CND received a boost when a working party, chaired by the Bishop of Salisbury published a report, *The Church and the Bomb*, which recommended 'unilateral steps within a multilateral process'. Here a Christian CND cross hangs on the barbed wire fence at Upper Heyford during 'Peace Pentecost', 1983.

Below 4,000 people simulate death from nuclear attack in a Glasgow square; 20,000 took part in the accompanying march, 2nd April 1983.

Right Youth CND Festival, May 1983. Thousands came to listen to the music and demonstrate support for nuclear disarmament in what was probably the most ambitious event ever organized by young people.

Below While big demonstrations attract attention, grassroots activity is the backbone of the movement. The efforts here by Hackney CND are paralleled each week by hundreds of groups throughout Britain.

Right Northern Ireland CND is non-sectarian and works in co-operation with both British and Irish CND. This picture was taken at the end of a 24-hour blockade of Bishopscourt, an advance warning radar station, June 1983.

Below Blockade at Greenham. Hundreds of singing and chanting women succeed in blocking the main entrance as a bus carrying workmen approaches the base.

Left Many feminists, encouraged by the Greenham example, organized women-only events and facilities.

Below A CND picket of the House of Commons which was supported by writers, artists, clergy, ex-Service people and others. On the left of the picture is the actress Susannah York; David Blunkett, Leader of Sheffield City Council; and the Rt. Rev. Tony Dumper, Bishop of Dudley.

Revelations of increasing radioactivity in the sea and on local beaches led to a loss of public confidence in the nuclear power industry. Membership of Greenpeace and Friends of the Earth grew quickly as a result of campaigns on the danger of nuclear power.

Above Greenpeace divers monitor nuclear waste emissions from the reprocessing plant at Sellafield (Windscale), on the Cumbrian coast.

Right The general election was held in June 1983. Public opinion polls consistently showed majority opposition to the government's nuclear policy on cruise missiles and Trident.

CND was determined to influence the election, not by standing candidates or supporting a particular party, but by increasing public awareness and opposition to nuclear weapons in a political context. Working through its specialist sections, the movement encouraged public meetings, a peace canvass, and questionnaires for candidates.

When the election came, however, CND was excluded from the debate. The Tories fought Labour on a charge of defencelessness, and the arguments about cruise and Trident were never put to the electorate.

In the nuclear election

vote for them.

You _can_ influence the Nuclear Arms question.

On June 9... It's _your_ choice

CND

In the ensuing months CND was determined to show that the re-election of Margaret Thatcher's government could not break the movement.

Right On a day when temperatures soared into the 80s°F, thousands of people formed a human chain linking the American and Russian embassies in London, in a plea for nuclear disarmament. Despite the heat, they waited cheerfully in line to pass a plastic globe from hand to hand along the two-mile route.

Below Women from many different countries form a chain outside the American embassy in Geneva, linking it to the Russian embassy, at the beginning of arms reduction talks in September 1983.

Opposite and above Scenes from the CND demonstration in London, October 1983. Opposition to the deployment of cruise missiles was as firm after the election as before it, and 400,000 people turned up to demonstrate this. Media coverage, as always, was mixed (see next page).

Annajoy David, then a leading member of Youth CND and one of the movement's most effective speakers, can be seen in the foreground of the picture opposite.

250,000 CND marchers jam heart of London

By CATHERINE STEVEN and CAROLE DAWSON

THE largest CND demonstration in two decades brought traffic in central London to a standstill yesterday. It was the last major protest against cruise missiles before their arrival at Greenham Common, planned for later this year.

At a rally in Hyde Park Mr Neil Kinnock was barracked by a group of black-flag-waving anarchists. A photographer was led away bleeding from a head wound as sticks, bottles and beer cans were thrown at police.

There were jeers and chants of "Politicians are liars" as Mr Kinnock, who had stood up on the platform to loud cheers, told demonstrators "This is the living movement, this is the movement for life."

He went on, "We were told that this is the movement of weakness and appeasement but we're saying this is the movement of people with the strength to care, and of people with the sense to know that nuclear weapons are made by human beings and must be dismantled by human beings."

About 250,000 demonstrators in two columns — one headed by Mr Michael Foot and the other by Mgr Bruce Kent and Mrs Joan Ruddock, the CND leaders — congregated on the Victoria Embankment. Mr Kinnock's wife Glenys and their two children, Stephen, 13, and Rachael, 11, were among the marchers.

The Coalition for Peace through Security staged a banner-and-placard counter-demonstration from the roof of their offices in Whitehall. Mr Tryggvi McDonald, 23-year-old son of Senator Lawrence McDonald, the American politician who was killed when Soviet jets shot down a South Korean airliner, spoke through a loud hailer

He asked: "If the Russians behaved in this way to dozens of innocent people in a defenceless aircraft, how do you think they would behave towards millions of people in a defenceless country?"

In Hyde Park, punks with coloured hairstyles watched entertainments as the marchers arrived. Roland Muldoon, the comedian, was joined on the stage by a police officer who warned him against his liberal use of four-letter words.

Scotland Yard said 25 arrests were made, mostly for minor offences.

Mrs Joan Ruddock, chairman of CND, announced plans for a new campaign. She said "Our aim is to ensure that the British people become aware of the immense threat posed by having the American-controlled weapons in this country."

More than 400 coaches, each carrying 50 demonstrators from the provinces, were booked into parking spaces at Hyde Park and 33 trains were chartered from British Rail. Each train cost nearly £3,000 to hire.

CND said its local groups had raised funds or collected fares from demonstrators.

OUR DIPLOMATIC STAFF writes: The "week of action" against cruise and Pershing II missiles staged by the West German Peace Movement, the largest in Europe, reached a climax yesterday as hundreds of thousands of demonstrators rallied in Bonn, Hamburg, West Berlin, Stuttgart and at the American base at Neu-Ulm.

Demonstrators outnumbered the total population in Bonn where 30,000 formed a "human chain" linking embassies.

Tens of thousands of anti-nuclear demonstrators rallied in Paris and Rome.

CND opposed by 67 pc

Only 23 per cent of people questioned in a Gallup Poll thought Britain should give up nuclear weapons unilaterally. Unilateralism was opposed by 67 per cent with 10 per cent "don't knows".

Among Labour supporters, 54 per cent opposed unilateralism. The poll was conducted for the Coalition for Peace Through Security.

Editorial Comment—P.18

Peace tide surge

A MASSIVE new upsurge in the British peace movement is being predicted after CND's triumphant rally against Cruise and Trident missiles on Saturday.

By HELEN BENNETT

400,000 people paralysed central London for the campaign's strongest ever protest against nuclear weapons, in what CND vice-chairman Roger Spillar described as "the sunrise for our peace movement."

They were part of a huge wave of peace activity that swept Western Europe and saw over 2½ million people take to the streets against nuclear weapons.

People from France, West Germany, Italy and Austria showed their determination to resist the deployment of US medium range nuclear missiles on their territories.

A million West Germans protested in Berlin, Bonn, Hamburg.

"The strength and creativity of Saturday's event will mark the beginning of a great resurgence in the peace movement and we will continue to campaign throughout the autumn to keep Cruise missiles out of the English countryside," she said.

Britain will see the mushrooming of direct action against Cruise and Trident as they are deployed, as CND concentrates its campaign against the missiles.

NEW CAMPAIGN

Ms. Ruddock announced the launching of a massive public information campaign to explain what the deployment of Cruise missiles will mean for the country.

Roger Spillar said: "Saturday's demonstration showed that a vast section of the British people are so opposed to Cruise and Pershing that they are prepared to come out into the streets

Blockade warning

CND leader Joan Ruddock warned yesterday that demonstrators would...

THE SUNDAY TIMES

Sunset for CND

Media coverage of CND's demonstration in October 1983. The *Sunday Times* leader (right) described CND as a failed campaign 'whose outer fringes could now turn to increasingly desperate activities'.

higher

FROM London's Hyde Park to Rome's San Giovanni Square, the nuclear disarmers had their day. But it was not the victorious eruption of a movement whose time has come. It was the last great gasp of a campaign which has clearly failed, and whose outer fringes could now turn to increasingly desperate activities to stop by violence what could not be stopped by democratic means.

The extent of their failure was underlined 24 hours before they began parading through western Europe's capitals. The socialist president of France and the right-wing prime minister of Britain ended their annual summit on Friday by declaring their joint support for maintaining their own independent nuclear deterrents and for the Nato decision to deploy Cruise and Pershing missiles in western Europe. Add to that the West German government's support for deployment and it is clear that the missiles are going in, no matter how much the disarmers protest.

Another mark of CND's failure is its new emphasis on Cruise rather than its original passion, unilateral nuclear disarmament. That was an argument it lost from stockbroker belt to council house estate on June 9, helping to ensure Labour's defeat on the way. As the marchers set out in London yesterday, they were reminded of that defeat by a Guardian poll showing that 77 per cent of the British want to maintain or improve our own nuclear deterrent. Hence the new emphasis on Cruise, of which the British are still suspicious, albeit less so than a year ago.

The Labour leader, Mr Neil Kinnock, who was the star turn in Hyde Park yesterday, has had to tailor his views to suit public opinion. In his short political career he has so far discarded his earlier sympathy for a neutral Britain (the Guardian poll found only 8 per cent in favour of that, with 73 per cent pro-Nato) and suppressed his own strong instincts in favour of unilateral nuclear disarmament (the poll showed only 16 per cent want that). But he can still rant against Cruise because public opinion is more finely balanced and Labour, for once, reasonably united.

Mr Kinnock's sudden enthusiasm for conventional defence, however, is hardly convincing. This is a country which has far fewer combat aircraft today than it had in 1939. The build-up of expensive conventional forces needed to make a non-nuclear Britain secure would be enormous. Does anyone seriously expect a future Kinnock government to devote more money to defence than Mrs Thatcher? Or is the new morality of the left to hide safely under the American nuclear umbrella, eschewing anything to do with such nasty weapons themselves?

The case for Cruise is strong, and the imminent arrival of the missiles a matter of some relief. Their deployment marks the failure of a major Soviet effort to decouple western Europe from the United States. As long as there was a chance of the "peace" protesters thwarting deployment, the Kremlin was never likely to take arms control talks seriously. The Russians had already deployed their SS-20s and had no reason to negotiate away an imbalance of terror which suited them. Now that Nato's missiles are going in the Soviets will no doubt sulk and even huff and puff about peppering eastern Europe with even more SS-20s.

But that is an arms race Nato need not run. Once Cruise and Pershing 2 are in place, the West will be well covered, no matter how many extra SS-20s Russia cares to deploy. The Kremlin knows that, which is why it is an empty threat. After a time, it will also realise that, with Cruise tilting the balance in the European theatre back to equilibrium, there is no alternative to large, negotiated nuclear arms reductions on both sides. If those who gathered in London yesterday had their way, that is a challenge the Soviet Union need never face.

Daily Mail, Tuesday, October 25, 1983

HOW MOTHERS LIKE ME ARE DRIVEN TO JOIN THE BIG PEACE DEMOS

SO were you there on October 22 ? Were you one of the huge crowd of 250,000 demonstrators thronging Hyde Park ?

And if you were not there, did you feel a little bit guilty about it ? Did some of that magnificent pre-rally CND propaganda get to you ?

Because it was indeed powerful propaganda. On Friday morning, the day before the demos, I and other mothers were delivering our tiny sons and daughters to their North London primary school.

This humdrum, happy, chattering little scene in the sunshine was briefly overshadowed by a sudden glimpse of apocalyptic terror in the form of two leaflets handed out to us at the gates.

The Cruise missile . . . target for CND fairytales. And (right) a concerned mother on the march.

This CND blackmail at our school gates . . .

by ANN LESLIE

Horrors

The first said : 'October 22. Where will you be ?' The second, from the Camden Labour Party, told us why we should be there on Saturday. Cruise missiles, due to be installed in December, will 'make nuclear war more likely. . . .'

And just in case we mothers were to preoccupied juggling with pushchairs and shopping-bags to understand the implications of that, the leaflets told us what would happen if a one megaton bomb was exploded over Trafalgar Square.

We live in the 'area north of 'London Zoo up to Hampstead 'Heath' and that would mean, among other horrors, '90 per cent. dead from blast (ruptured guts, crushed bones).'

It didn't of course mention that the Soviets already have over 350 SS20s installed, each with three warheads, two-thirds of which are targeted on Western Europe. Information like that might 'confuse' us mothers outside the school gates.

Nor did it mention that most members of unofficial peace groups in Eastern Europe — those not controlled for propaganda purposes by the Soviet authorities — are bitterly opposed to the unilateralist and neutralist ideas of CND.

These Eastern Europeans know the realities of Soviet power, and they know that the West can only hope to succeed in disarmament negotiations if it negotiates from a position of strength.

The message handed out at the school gates had to be kept 'unconfused' by such 'irrelevant' facts.

And so, yes, those leaflets did have a powerful emotional kick. As I watched my adored little five-year-old cheerfully hurrying into class with her best friend, I felt a sudden lurch in my stomach.

Those two merry little souls, millions of innocents like them — 'ruptured guts, crushed bones'. Please God, no !

Declined

So why didn't I join that march on Saturday ? Don't I care ?

Well, it so happens that I was there—not as a demonstrator but as an observer. I was making a film report for Channel 4 on the demonstration which CND now claims is 'proof' that the peace movement has just lost its battle.

Unfortunately for them, so that same reason has come, deep in polls. Just look at all these people here. How can you say we aren't a majority ? Where are all those people who you say don't agree with us ?'

Sitting at home, I pointed out, or visiting friends, watching football, or out shopping—doing all the things most people do on Saturdays.

I had assumed that everyone in that crowd on Saturday actually knew what they were demonstrating about. But did they ?

Oh sure, they were, as everyone told me earnestly, demonstrating 'in favour of peace and against nuclear war'. Well, you'd have to be criminally insane not to be in favour of peace and against nuclear war. So let's try to take it beyond the infants' class level.

The demonstrators thought that if the West didn't frighten

troying a hardened silo and cannot destroy a nuclear submarine out at sea, is hardly an ideal weapon.)

Nor is there any illusion at NATO or SHAPE headquarters (where last week I sat through many discussions with men with titles like Head of Nuclear Planning) that America could fight a limited nuclear war in Europe.

As General Rogers, the American Supreme Allied Commander, Europe, said : 'The Soviets have said that any American weapon system being fired at Soviet soil will be cause for her to attack the United States with strategic weapons.'

How many of the people in the crowd of 250,000 have been told any of this by CND ? Very few.

Alas, some of those didn't even seem to know the difference between 'unilateralist' and 'multilateralist'. One nice, earnest young man told me he was there because he was a 'multilateralist'.

Outbreak

But this, I pointed out, was a demonstration in favour of 'unilateralism'. His response was a look of utter bafflement.

Many in the crowd used the demonstration to promote a whole variety of separate causes. Like the seller of the Hard-Left newspaper who told me we must 'defend the Soviet Union against Western imperialism.'

Like those who wanted solar heating in homes. Like the Hare Krishna people who said that meat-eating was the cause of nuclear war.

And like the Greenham women, who were collecting money to finance a 'permanent' peace headquarters.

Not so long ago, they were telling me that the arrival of the first Cruise missile would mean the outbreak of nuclear Armageddon. Since the end of the world is nigh in a few weeks, it seemed odd, to say the least, to ask for money to set up a 'permanent' headquarters.

So all of you who have felt a twinge of guilt about not 'being there on October 22' — forget it. The majority of those who were there were well-meaning, hopelessly muddled, easily exploited people who've come to

opinion does not exist as a political force ?

Oh yes, that worried some people. But most people said they were sure that public opinion in the Soviet bloc would eventually influence the rulers in the Kremlin into more peaceable and 'accountable' ways.

No use pointing out that public opinion as expressed by the people of Hungary, East Germany, Czechoslovakia, Poland and Afghanistan has only influenced the Kremlin into greater spasms of repression and cruelty.

Destroy

Presumably most of those at the demonstration were convinced by CND's propaganda that Cruise missiles are being deployed only because they're the sort of offensive weapon which the West intends to use in a pre-emptive first strike against the Russians.

(In fact, Cruise, whose launch-on-warning system requires several hours' preparation before firing, is essentially a retaliatory 'second strike' weapon. A missile which takes hours to prepare, which is incapable of des-

---

Media attacks on CND continue. Teachers for Peace and Bruce Kent are particular targets.

This battle for your child's mind

by Rodney Tyler

now stood in the way of the total politicisation of the capital's children.

The fact is that most parents, throughout the country, would be horrified if they realised how, even in the basic routine subjects, such as English, History and Science, their sons and daughters are being indoctrinated.

Take a look at the methods employed in sample lessons in at least one school:

An English lesson is based on how the language of the nuclear age is used by the media to condition ordinary people into accepting Cruise missiles.

Then the teacher takes a headline from the sports pages: 'Hammers massacre Coventry in five-goal blitz.' He uses it as the starting point for a discussion which moves on to deplore the way newspapers and TV glory in war and distort the views of those who believe in peace.

Science, before lunch, is easier. The Physics master, in defiance of a request from the Minister of Education, gives the pupils the full benefit of his personal conviction that American possession of a nuclear arsenal is a one-way suicide trip for mankind.

History, in the afternoon, is a study, through books supplied to the school by Novosti, the Soviet Press agency, of Russia's peaceloving intentions over the last 30 years, compared with Western warmongering.

A fantasy ? Not the sort of school you would dream of letting your child attend ?

No. It is fact. And you might soon have no choice but to send your child to such a school.

For there is at least one comprehensive school in Britain where each one of those sample lessons—or ones similar—has already taken place. And there are at least a dozen major local

released for special courses in how to combat racism.

Another London head described a visit from one of the proliferating 'advisers' who demanded to know why Irish politics, history, literature, and music were not being taught to the Irish children in his school.

The visitor accused him of 'not co-operating' when he pointed out that he had 30 different nationalities in the school and if he discriminated in favour of one minority he would have to favour them all.

But he sees as far more sinister the question he and ILEA's 170 comprehensive heads were forced to answer recently : 'Do you recognise the role of the "hidden curriculum" in political education ?'

He told me : 'It was rather like being asked if I had stopped beating my wife. If I said yes it would have meant that I was secretly indoctrinating my children, if I said no it meant I was refusing to do so. Either way I would be open to attack.'

The hidden curriculum is another way, in Left-Wing eyes, of influencing children. Put bluntly, it means taking every opportunity as it arises in normal lessons to put across your political message.

It is this sinister move, which ILEA—Britain's biggest authority—is poised to introduce. Thus, both overtly and covertly they plan a massive programme of indoctrination.

Printed advice on how to get rid of uncooperative heads which circulates secretly among some of these groups includes such gems as :

● Hold sudden meetings at the most difficult times for the head and his staff.

● Prolong meetings unnecessarily and harass officials of the Board into resignation — then put your own people into their positions.

In Britain's biggest teachers' union, the National Union of Teachers, more than 10 per cent. of delegates at the annual conferences come from just one of the extreme Left-Wing groups operating within the educational system.

But what he feared most of all was the attempt by the notorious Inner London Education Authority to foist on him those that they wanted to, in line with its far-left leadership.

This school year he will be ordered to give more status to

"Monsignor Kent is out but he asked me to take a message"

CND: IS IT ALL A RUSSIAN CON TRICK?

By MARJORY DAVIDSON

Moscow's making fools of our ban the bomb brigade

THE 19 Very Important Visitors were welcomed to Moscow in the style of Heads of State.

Police escorted their motorcade as it swept through red lights on the way from Sheremitovo Airport to a downtown hotel.

Visits to the Bolshoi Ballet, the old Czarist capital, Leningrad and the fabled cities of Tashkent and Samarkand were on the programme.

And it was red carpet treatment all the way.

The cost of this 10 day jaunt? Nothing—save the £190 cut-price air fare from London.

Who were the lucky 19? Not pop stars, or soccer players or even astronauts.

They were members of the Campaign for Nuclear Disarmament and fellow sympathisers. Lord Brockway, co-

chairman of the World Disarmament Campaign, led the party which included respected pacifists Dr Malcolm Dando, of Bradford University's School of Peace Studies, Richard Keeble, editor of The Teacher, and Father Owen Hardwicke, of Iay Christi, the Roman Catholic Disarmament lobby.

They had come to Moscow to talk peace.

But like the hundreds of thousands of ban-the-bomb marchers through-

out Europe, they were and are, tragically, just dupes.

They are part of a campaign that is orchestrated and financed by the Soviet Union with the direct purpose of weakening the West, her resolve and her strength, while Russia continues to build up the most fearsome military machine in history.

Take that starry-eyed journey last March. The Russians quickly showed

their visitors that they wanted others to talk about peace. They want others to disarm.

The naive band of travellers were campaigning for Britain to scrap all nuclear weapons. When they hesitantly asked the Kremlin to make a possible ten per cent reduction in its nuclear arsenal, the reply was a brutal " Niet."

In Britain, the ban-the-bomb campaign is booming. Membership has increased from 3,000 to 37,000 in 18 months and includes many idealistic young people.

Last October, more than 150,000 people from all over Britain attended the biggest demonstration in London since the heady days of the Sixties.

Brezhnev flew from Moscow to meet the 1,000 Soviet-subsidised delegates in Sofia.

Labour MPs present included Roy Hughes (Newport), James Lamond (Oldham East), Andrew Bennett (Stockport North), William Wilson (Coventry SE) and Alf Lomas (Euro MP London NE).

Alex Kitson, executive officer of the Transport and General Workers' Union, was also among the guests.

In Britain, as CND membership has grown, a Left-wing takeover has emer..., the top.

Idealists have been replaced by militants with

potent Euro-Communist connections.

They seek a power base in Britain. They aim to get it by exploiting the fear and horror felt by decent men and women at the idea of nuclear war.

They have formed special sections — Youth CND and Christian CND —to extend their sphere of influence.

They are especially active in trying to persuade trade unions to affiliate to CND.

These are the facts to remember when next you are impressed by lovers on the marches Moscow-style.

LEFTIES WHO RUN PEACE CAMPAIGN

THESE are the people behind the CND in Britain.

89

Right The government meanwhile had something to hide, and Sarah Tisdall, Foreign Office clerk, leaked it to *The Guardian:* Michael Heseltine, Secretary of State for Defence, planned to mislead the House of Commons about the arrival of cruise missiles at Greenham.

Ms Tisdall pleaded guilty and was convicted under the Official Secrets Act. She was sent to prison for six months.

Below The first flight of cruise missiles arrives at Greenham Common. Women wept in anger and frustration, but no-one in the peace movement was prepared to accept defeat.

CND plan shooting of a 'peace martyr'

By Maj.-Gen. EDWARD FURSDON
Defence Correspondent

DESPITE the fact of the cruise missiles' arrival at Greenham Common, there are still volunteers who have agreed—if it is in the interests of the continued campaign — to be shot and wounded by their colleagues, preferably with American calibre bullets, said a source associated with C N D.

Hopefully a suitable "incident" could then be staged in an attempt to blame the security forces.

Such a bizarre contingency plan of peace martyrdom, they feel, would be their unique contribution to their cause.

There are a number of other somewhat way-out plans still pending, the source said, among the dedicated "peacenics," depending on what the overall campaign for 1984, and any training deployment plans of cruise missiles the Defence Ministry might have, might demand.

These include the silent infiltration of C N D supporters into the Greenham Common base by balloon, para-ascending or hang-glider. Once inside the base by these or any other means, the source said, recordings of, or simulated small arms firing—in the absence of real fire by the defending forces—could be used to stimulate speculation and confusion especially among the Press and media.

Another ploy

The illegal donning of official uniforms to aid passage through official cordons during a provoked melée of suitably staged demonstrations is yet another ploy to be kept "in the bag."

The latter, equipped with stretchers and fake casualties, might arouse little notice from the authorities during suitably designed chaos, the fanatics feel.

More sophisticated disruption techniques under consideration, include breaking into the security forces' radio networks—using the correct procedures.

But, perhaps the most sinister security incident of all, the source said, was the leaking by a young engineer "mole" of drawings of Greenham Common buildings and duct circuits to an attractive C N D woman supporter with whom he had hoped to establish a relationship.

Although some of the buildings shown were not sensitive, nevertheless to any professional terrorist planning an attack on a target complex, such information is useful to him as indicating where not to waste his time.

As 1983 drew to a close, there was further press hysteria calling into question CND's commitment to non-violence.

Left The 'peace martyr' story alludes to Michael Heseltine's warning that armed guards might shoot protesters who entered security areas. No source has been found for this story.

Below On 20th December, there were two small, spontaneous and non-violent demonstrations by London CND groups, in response to the first mobilization of cruise missile convoys on British roads, while the previous Saturday the IRA had bombed Harrods. (Four months later the Press Council ruled in favour of CND, calling the headline 'irresponsible in the extreme'.)

Police anger as demos take men off bomb watch duty

NO ENTRY: anti-nuclear demonstrators block the highway at the junction of Mile End and Whitechapel roads. Picture: DAVID HOFFMAN

CND 'HOLDING HANDS WITH IRA'

by Bob Graham

POLICE angrily criticised spontaneous CND demonstrators in London today for "holding hands with the IRA bombers."

Two anti-Cruise demos were held—at Trafalgar Square and in the Mile End Road in East London—to protest against the redeployment of nuclear missiles from Greenham Common.

Culpable

But more than 200 police officers who had been called into central London to boost the watch for terrorist bombers were immediately reassigned to handle the surprise demonstrations.

A police inspector at Trafalgar Square said: "These people are not helping their cause at a time like this.

"They are taking away the effectiveness of drafting in extra resources to combat the bombers.

"We are here watching these people demonstrate rather than doing the job we should be. If another bomb goes off in Central London these people can be held culpable. They are simply holding hands with "the bombers."

The CND said the protest had been organised at two hours' notice and John Clark, chairman of Bromley CND, said: "It's not a matter of the police being angry with us. It's more important that we should be angry that Cruise missiles are being redeployed around the English countryside and threatening the lives of us all."

The organisers did not give police details of their plans. The heavy presence of nearly 150 officers at Trafalgar Square prevented the CND marching along Whitehall.

As they gathered for the three-hour protest they were warned they could be arrested because they did not have permission to hold the demonstration.

At Mile End, 15 people who halted traffic were arrested. Twelve women and three men lay down in the west-bound carriageway and blocked the road for nearly 25 minutes.

THE STANDARD

Thursday, March 29, 1984   18p   *Incorporating the* Evening News

CITY PRICES

Protesters lie down in path of lorries

DEMO BLOCKS CRUISE CONVOY

Report : BOB GRAHAM
Picture : AUBREY HART

GREENHAM COMMON demonstrators used their bodies as human shields to block a convoy of Cruise missile launchers as it went on a secret exercise today.

Police clashed with several hundred demonstrators as the 26-vehicle convoy was brought to a halt outside the main gates of the military base in Berkshire.

Two vehicles owned by peace protesters were driven in front of the convoy, forcing a missile launcher lorry on to a grass verge. It smashed down a church sign and a picket fence.

At least four Greenham women threw themselves in front of other vehicles in the convoy, which were not carrying live missiles, forcing them to brake sharply to avoid running over them.

One male protester tried unsuccessfully to ram the convoy with a white Volkswagen and another dumped his car in its path. Then the driver tried to run back and lie in front of the convoy.

At one stage during the 120-mile military exercise along main roads, including the M4 and the A34, demonstrators drove their cars at high speeds the wrong way along dual carriageways to overtake the Cruise convoy.

The Greenham women claimed "a victory of sorts" for halting the convoy and proving that it could be stopped on public roads.

But Assistant Chief Constable Wyn Jones of Thames Valley Police, criticised the protesters for "reckless and dangerous behaviour that put other lives at great risk".

Many of the Greenham women claimed they were punched, kicked and beaten by more than 100 police officers at the scene.

The drama began shortly after midnight when the Cruise convoy left the main gates of the air base and headed to RAF Lyneham in Wiltshire.

Immediately the women notified sympathetic CND and peace groups in Hampshire, Berkshire, Wiltshire and Buckinghamshire. Within an hour, many had gathered outside the gates to wait for the returning convoy.

Assistant Chief Constable Jones defended the huge police presence by saying: "The operation was to ensure the safe passage along the highway of vehicles that had every right to be there.

"It was perfectly obvious that the sole intention of the women here was to prevent lawful and rightful passage of the vehicles along the highway, and

Continued Page 2, Col 1

FIRM ACTION : police hold down a man who tried to sit down in front of the convoy.

Top left The Ministry of Defence had claimed that cruise missiles would melt into the countryside. The peace movement was determined they should not, and established an elaborate telephone network involving Greenham women and local activists to track any movement of convoys from the Greenham base.

Above Local councils and the Ministry of Defence took repeated court actions to remove the women from Greenham Common. They succeeded in removing their caravan homes, but with typical ingenuity the women constructed these 'benders' of branches and polythene.

Left A member of Northern Ireland CND, dressed up as St Patrick, is escorted away from the dawn blockade of Bishopscourt, March 1984.

84

CND decided during 1984 to highlight the presence of American military bases and facilities in Britain, then numbering 135. Hundreds of groups took action at local sites.

Right Christian CND witness at Upper Heyford USAF base, Ash Wednesday 1984.

Below The common struggle against cruise and Pershing II missiles throughout Western Europe led to increasing co-operation between national peace movements, and participation in each other's demonstrations.

West Midlands CND organized an international festival which included representatives from both East and West, under the slogan, 'No Cruise; No Pershing; No SS20s'.

free europe from nuclear weapons

CND COVENTRY MAY 26

March - Rally - Concert   Saturday May 26
Assemble 11.30 am at Edgwick Park, Foleshill Road

Above CND airborne.

Left 'Die-in' in Amsterdam, 7th May 1984.

Left A silent vigil of nearly 1,000 pensioners (some of them in their 80s) at Greenham, 20th March 1984.

The 'nuclear winter' is a scientific hypothesis which postulates that, after a major nuclear exchange, the sky will be so darkened by debris that the northern hemisphere will freeze, destroying all remaining life.

Below The plinth is prepared in Trafalgar Square for the rally at the end of the biggest march of 1984 – protesting the visit of Ronald Reagan to Britain. Increasingly CND was drawing attention to the cost of the arms race, and the needs of the Third World.

The plinth placard shows Reagan carrying a briefcase, said to contain secret codes enabling him to order the start of a nuclear war from anywhere in the world. Irish CND ran a striking poster campaign against his visit to the Republic, entitled 'Leave the briefcase at home'.

Right 'A million sandcastles for peace', a summer action conducted by CND members at Rhyl in North Wales.

Below Taken from inside the fence, this photograph shows an army video being made of protesters at RAF Chilwell, a proposed US Army Vehicle Depot, 1st July 1984.

Bottom right A 10-day protest at Greenham, September 1984. Women came from all over the world. Here Kay from Bromley and Orpington CND talks to Ruth from York.

The government's decision to replace Polaris by Trident (at a cost of £10,000m) was a compromise arrangement with the US. Britain would buy the missiles from America, produce its own warheads at Aldermaston and Burghfield, and build its own submarines.

The contract for the latter was awarded to Vickers' ailing Barrow shipyards, and offered job security in an area hard-hit by unemployment. CND argued that taxpayers' money could be used to create alternative jobs, and that it was not a case of 'Trident or the dole'. To pursue this idea, CND donated £12,000 to a local trade union project researching alternative plans for the Barrow shipyards.

Opposite centre Trade unionists pledge support for CND. From left to right are Brian Nicholson and Walter Greendale of the TGWU, and Rodney Bickerstaffe of NUPE, 24th October 1984.

Opposite bottom Anti-Trident demonstration at Barrow-in-Furness, 27th October 1984. Shapua Kaukunga of SWAPO (the South West Africa People's Organization) makes the link between the British government's purchase of illegally mined uranium from Namibia, and the nuclear weapons programme.

Right Thousands of activists from all over Britain came to Barrow-in-Furness to demonstrate against Trident.

Right Thousands of activists from all over Britain came to Barrow-in-Furness to demonstrate against Trident.

Below Marching past the great steel doors of the plant where parts for the submarine are being built.

Above During 1984 attention focused increasingly
on Molesworth, designated as the second cruise
missile site, in rural Cambridgeshire. Small peace
camps were already well-established and plans had
been laid to frustrate the construction work which
was due to begin at any time. Meanwhile some of the
fields were planted, and building began on a peace
chapel.

Opposite top This harvest for the hungry at
'Rainbow Fields Village', Molesworth, linked
disarmament with famine in Africa. The lorry is
carrying grain destined for Eritrea. Some of it was
grown locally, the rest donated by people from all over
Britain, October 1984.

Right Sowing winter wheat. The crop was never
harvested as the land was enclosed by the Ministry of
Defence in the following February.

From 1981 onwards, CND's high media profile and level of activity had attracted international attention. Co-operation based on a policy of strict non-alignment was fostered with sister movements in Western Europe, the USA, Canada, Japan, Australia, and many other countries. Delegations were sent to Eastern Europe and the USSR. Here the first CND delegation visits the People's Republic of China, November 1984.

Opposite top In January 1985, Lawyers for Nuclear Disarmament set up a tribunal to test the legality of nuclear weapons. Here solicitor Geoffrey Bindman reads a message from Professor Tairov of the Soviet Union, who was refused entry to Britain to attend the tribunal. On the platform, from left to right, are Nobel laureates Sean McBride, Professor Dorothy Hodgkin and Professor Maurice Wilkins.

Right Meanwhile, in the dead of night and with an unprecedented show of force, 1,500 soldiers and hundreds of police removed 100 peace campaigners from Molesworth, and hastily erected a barbed wire fence, 6th February 1985. The cost was estimated at £1 million.

85

Troops clear peace camp from Cruise missile base

Standard Picture: MIKE LAWN

WELL DONE, CHAPS : Michael Heseltine surv eys the new 7¼-mile barbed wire fence today.

KEEP OUT!

Above The newly erected fence at Molesworth is soon hung with placards, as Ministry of Defence police guard the partly built peace chapel – later to be demolished.

Right Blockading an entrance to RAF Molesworth, 10th February 1985.

Top Revelations that government civil defence plans in the run-up to a nuclear war included the arrest of persons deemed 'subversive' led to groups of actors, musicians, trade unionists, nurses and ex-Services CND 'giving themselves up' at Scotland Yard, 26th February 1985. Paul Weller, of Style Council, and playwright Harold Pinter can be seen in the front row.

Left Welsh activists in Cardiff mark the anniversary of the Nuclear-free Declaration in Wales, February 1985.

Above West Midlands CND protest outside the offices of US Gold Ltd, manufacturers of a computer game called 'Raid over Moscow'.

Left In March 1985 a group of women toured Britain, campaigning against the militarization of the Pacific Ocean and particularly the human cost of nuclear testing by Western powers. One is seen here addressing a meeting of Bristol CND.

Bottom left The peace chapel at Molesworth, Easter 1985. Bob Geldof's Live Aid for Africa inspires the peace movement.

Below Singing nuns gently confront the police as Christian CND supporters encircle the Ministry of Defence in Whitehall, 27th May 1985.

Bottom Cruisewatch members sit in the path of a cruise missile support convoy, delaying it for an hour, as it heads for a deployment site on Salisbury Plain.

Far left Daily evictions by bailiffs, employed by Newbury District Council, resulted in great hardship, and meant that fewer women lived permanently at the Greenham camp. However the protest and the spirit continued.

Left The network which alerts Cruisewatch members to follow and intercept cruise convoys can also be used to encourage CND groups in the gentler art of hanging banners on railings to publicize the convoys.

The 40th anniversary of the Hiroshima and Nagasaki bombs, on 6th August 1985, was marked all over the world by peace groups and nuclear-free authorities. The Soviet Union began a unilateral moratorium on nuclear testing, and invited the United States to conclude a comprehensive test ban.

These survivors from Hiroshima were invited to London as part of an extensive peace programme organized by the Greater London Council.

Here in Brighton, as in many other cities, 'shadows' appeared on the pavement overnight, in memory of those who were vapourized by the Hiroshima and Nagasaki bombs, and whose indelible marks were left on Japanese pavements and buildings. August 1985.

Opposite Civil disobedience, accepted as an integral part of CND campaigning in the 1980s, was taken up by increasing numbers of people.

Top left The Snowball campaigners, seen here at RAF Chilwell, are pledged to undertake symbolic wirecutting until Britain makes some progress towards multilateral nuclear disarmament.

Top right Local support for the Greenham women continues.

Above Fence cutting at Greenham Common, 8th September 1985.

112

Opposite top A child's eye view of a US Poseidon submarine – the replacement for Polaris at the Holy Loch. The submarine can be seen more clearly in the bottom picture.

Above Protesters arrested inside the security fence at the British Polaris base at Faslane.

Left 'Rally for the human race' – part of a huge march organized by CND in London, 26th October 1985.

'Rally for the human race', 26th October 1985. In front can be seen Bruce
Kent, General Secretary of CND 1980-5, his successor Meg Beresford,
Glenys Kinnock, a long-time member of CND, and Sardul Gill, an Ealing
local councillor.

Opposite, top and bottom 6th February 1986, on the anniversary of the
construction of the fence, 6,000 people maintain a total blockade of RAF
Molesworth – despite the freezing conditions!

REAGAN JETS BLITZ LIBYA!

GADDAFI: Accused of giving
help to terror groups

Gaddafi targets blasted in war on terrorists

By NIGEL FREEDMAN

PRESIDENT Reagan launched his "revenge" blitz on Libya early today.

American jets roared in to blast "Mad Dog" dictator Gaddafi's capital of Tripoli.

A US correspondent reported: "Tripoli is under attack."

He said heavy smoke was rising from the centre of the city.

White House spokesman Larry Speakes said in Washington that U.S. forces had conducted air strikes against what he called "terrorist-related" targets in Libya.

He added that the U.S. war-planes that conducted the attacks were returning to their bases.

Speakes said "every effort has been made" to avoid hitting civilian targets.

REAGAN: Ordered bomb blitz
on Libyan terror targets.

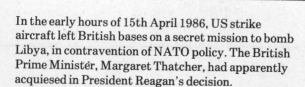

In the early hours of 15th April 1986, US strike aircraft left British bases on a secret mission to bomb Libya, in contravention of NATO policy. The British Prime Minister, Margaret Thatcher, had apparently acquiesed in President Reagan's decision.

There were numerous civilian casualties, including Gaddafi's adopted daughter.

CND officers immediately protested at the US embassy, and that evening called a candlelight vigil in Downing Street.

Right Demonstrations continued throughout the week and culminated in one of the largest ever civil disobedience actions, in front of the US embassy. In the foreground are Bruce Kent, Paul Johns (Chairperson of CND) and Joan Ruddock.

Opposite Here the protesters crowd into Oxford Street, and again sit down 'illegally', 19th April 1986. Many demonstrators complained of rough handling by the police *(bottom right)*.

Above Local CND groups organized protests against the Libya raid at US bases all over Britain, like this one at Fairford in Gloucestershire.

Below Many people felt moved to speak out, write letters or join demonstrations for the first time in their lives.

In 1985 CND had decided that, while opinion polls continued to show majority opposition to cruise and Trident, only *minority* support existed for total British unilateral nuclear disarmament. As a result the Campaign was given a new direction. CND's 'basic case' was advanced in a series of coordinated and extended public information campaigns, launched in spring 1986.

Right Bristol CND pioneer the concept of 'basic case' campaigning.

Below The huge London party, designed to attract maximum media attention through the participation of a galaxy of well-known supporters, was eclipsed by the bombing of Libya two days earlier.

But local group activities were well publicized. South-East Region CND launched their 'basic case' campaign with a sponsored bike ride to Brighton, April 1986.

Above To publicize the 'basic case' in Sevenoaks, they got off their bikes and picked up their bags, April 1986.

Right In Leeds they read out a roll call listing all the 50,000 nuclear weapons in the world.

Opposite, top In Blackpool they scaled the walls of the Town Hall.

Opposite, centre and bottom Trade union involvement in CND greatly increased in the 1980s, with most major unions affiliating to the campaign.

Their activity was centred around arms conversion, the reallocation of resources from warfare to welfare, and their opposition to the concept of civil defence against nuclear war. Many trade unions participated in 'basic case' campaigning.

NUCLEAR WAR GAMES

NUPE, NALGO, TGWU COHSE, GMBATU, TU CND, FBU

For us as public service workers, in the health and fire services and with local councils, the choice is clear: either we take part in the Government's Civil Defence charades — planning post holocaust menus, evacuating hospitals and running exercises in underground control centres — or we explain clearly to fellow workers and the public the reality that our emergency services could not cope with even a limited nuclear attack.

NO THANKS

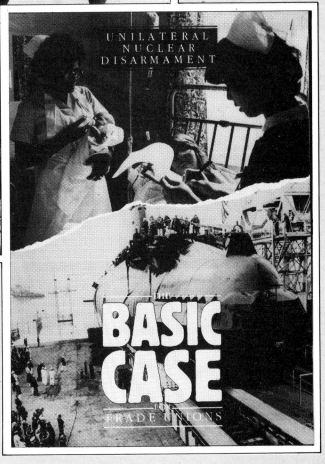

UNILATERAL NUCLEAR DISARMAMENT

BASIC CASE

TRADE UNIONS

ON THE POWER OF NUCLEAR ENERGY

ATOM CLOUD COVERS UK

THE Russian radiation cloud last night covered the whole of Britain as UK nuclear power stations faced a shut-down in a pay row.

A threatened walkout by electricians and engineers would hit safety inspections and repair work forcing some plants to close.

- American scientists, based in Britain, flew to Russia yesterday to carry out radiation tests in Moscow following the Chernobyl disaster.
- The disaster was blamed on human error by the Russians yesterday.
- Iodine anti-radiation tablets can make people impotent, the health department warned. Worried parents have been trying to get the tablets for their children but experts say the contamination levels in Britain are low.

Chernobyl nuclear plant USSR. Reactors exploded last week causing massive amounts of radiation to escape

USSR

EVERY DOT ON THE MAP SHOWS A NUCLEAR PLANT

THE NUCLEAR AGE

Drawing by DON ROBERTS

"jacket" round its nuclear power stations. It decided to save money and not to do it.

The West German jacket, for example, is so tough that a jumbo jet could crash full on it without smashing it.

Could Chernobyl happen here — at Dounreay, or say, Dungeness?

Yes, it could, and there's no sense in ducking the fact. It is a remote, theoretical, almost impossible possibility.

Everything went wrong at Chernobyl.

Control

It was the wrong system in the wrong place operated by the wrong Government.

The Russians took a chance and the chance didn't come off.

Nuclear power can keep the world warm — or it can incinerate it. It must be caged. It must be kept under control.

The price of its energy is eternal vigilance.

SO FAR, WE HAVEN'T HAD IT.

THIS is the world of nuclear power. According to the latest offical figures Britain has 38 reactors, the United States 93 and disaster-struck USSR 51.

The map shows that the bulk of nuclear energy plants are in Europe, USA and Russia. There are very few in the Third World and none in Australia.

Europe, USA and Russia have all had accidents — at Windscale (now Sellafield) in 1957, at America's Three Mile Island in 1979 and now at Chernobyl.

In Britain we rely on gas-cooled reactors. But the Central Electricity Board wants to build a water-cooled model at Sizewell.

The ill-fated Chernobyl reactor was water-cooled.

Planners say the British one will be safer.

On 26th April 1986, a nuclear power station at Chernobyl in the Soviet Union suffered the world's worst nuclear accident. Soviet authorities fought the raging reactor fire in secret until escaping radiation, registering in the West, forced them to announce the disaster. Media coverage in the West concentrated on the sensational aspects *(above)*.

Opposite bottom CND and Friends of the Earth register an immediate response at the Department of Energy.

STOP DrINKING rAIN WATER SAY BOFFINS

Atom fall-out alert

DISASTER IN RUSSIA

NUCLEAR experts last night warned country folk: Don't drink rainwater.

The alert was sounded by government scientists monitoring radiation fall-out from the Russ

They ad
campers a
with rai
streams, v

It was
since the
down clou
Britain tho
admitted t
health risk

Scotland
England a
were singl

NUKE

FALLOUT from the stricken Chernobyl reactor is greater than all the previous atmospheric nuclear tests put together, radiation experts said yesterday. And it is 2,000 times stronger than that from the first atomic bomb dropped on Hiroshima in 1945.

SPOT

NUKE

*THE R
radiatio
1,000 t
than th
Three
accident
the to
nuclear
Gunnar
said ye
warnec
8,000 p
get canc
Chernob*

ATOM CLOUD LAMB SHOCK

BRITISH wives may have served radioactive lamb to their families following the Russian nuclear disaster, the Government admitted yesterday.

Lamb carcases tested in slaughterhouses have shown levels of radiation above acceptable levels. Grass affected by the Chernobyl cloud is to blame.

By BILL GREIG

The findings were revealed as the Government imposed a 21-day ban on the movement and slaughter of sheep in Cumbria and North Wales.

It puts 14 million animals into effective quarantine and could mean ruin for some hill farm

Sc
abou
isoto

A

contaminated lamb may already have slipped through the net, Agriculture Minister Michael Jopling tried to allay public fears.

He said the amount that may have reached the butcher's slabs "would be very marginal indeed." And there was no danger to health.

In March 1983 President Reagan made a speech advocating a defensive shield for America against nuclear weapons – the so-called Strategic Defence Initiative, or 'Star Wars'.

The fantasy began to become a reality when millions of dollars were voted for research. British firms were invited to take part, and here Plaid Cymru MP Dafydd Elis Thomas, Labour MPs Ann Clwyd and Gavin Strang, and Liberal MP Jim Wallace join the Star Wars character Darth Vader outside the House of Commons, to protest against British participation, 8th July 1986.

The Glastonbury festival has grown into a legend. Organized by farmer
Michael Eavis and enthusiastically supported by CND volunteers, the
four-day peace festival has annually given around 20,000 people an
opportunity to enjoy the best of rock and folk music in aid of CND.

OFFENCE OF THE REALM

HOW PEACE CAMPAIGNERS GET BUGGED

Gillian Reeve and Joan Smith

On 29th July 1986, CND took the government to court. This was the result of information brought to light in a television programme made for Channel 4, in which an ex-MI5 agent, Cathy Massiter, revealed secret service surveillance of key people in CND, including phone tapping.

On the basis of Cathy Massiter's testimony, CND took legal action in the High Court.

Above CND already had hundreds of complaints from members about telephone and mail interference, and other inexplicable events. Since no redress exists in the British courts for such issues, a decision was taken to publish the material, and also to lodge a complaint with the European Commission on Human Rights.

Fundraising is always a priority.

Top Collecting money, selling literature and exchanging views – essential local group activity, whatever the weather.

Centre Scene at the CND fair in Bristol, July 1986.

Above left Tom Conti, the actor, and George Galloway, Director of War on Want, accompany Bruce Kent at the end of his march across Britain, from Faslane to Burghfield. Over £100,000 was raised for CND, and for projects in Nicaragua and Eritrea.

Also in the photograph are Wendy Pullen and David Rumsey, who organized the route.

Families' peaceful protests turn away scientists

The nuclear stand-off

We'll be back say men in dumping tests

FAMILIES turned out yesterday to prevent their villages being tested for the dumping of nuclear waste.

Calmly, they formed human chains of young and old. Quietly, the scientists and engineers who had arrived to begin the test-drilling drove away.

The peaceful protests at the three villages had succeeded. But the men from NIREX, the Government nuclear waste agency, warned that they would be back.

They are now likely to ask a court for injunctions to get them on to the sites.

At Fulbeck in Lincolnshire, a team of six NIREX engineers turned up at 11 a.m. to find a human wall of men, women and children at the main entrance, while another was barred with concrete blocks.

Vigil

The trucks drove off, only to try again four hours later. The protesters had then grown to 400, and the NIREX men again went away.

At Killingholme on Humberside, the engineers' Land-Rover drove up to find the way block by 150 demonstrators—and, after a few moments, drove off.

The protesters began a round-the-clock vigil to watch for the engineers' return and promised to use cars and farm vehicles to block the site.

At Elstow in Bedfordshire, about 75 people of all ages sat cross-legged and refused to move as the NIREX convoy drew up. The convoy left. There was no trouble at any of the three sites.

Test-drilling at a fourth village—Bradwell in Essex—is not due to start for two weeks.

The four have been chosen as possible sites for the burial of low to intermediate level radioactive waste from nuclear power stations, hospital laboratories and industry—much of it contaminated clothing.

NIREX trucks drive off after meeting a wall of protesters at Fulbeck yesterday

In August 1986, the government named four possible new locations for nuclear waste burial, the result of its plans to expand the nuclear power industry, and continuing problems with waste storage at Sellafield/Windscale.

Effective protests were mounted at all four of the named sites, at Fulbeck in Lincolnshire, Killingholme on Humberside, Elstow in Bedfordshire and Bradwell in Essex.

CND decided that the second stage of the 'basic case' campaign should be devoted to the British nuclear deterrent, the British bomb.

While the position of the government on this issue was apparently immovable, all the opposition parties were busy clarifying or developing their policy, and CND was determined to make its presence felt at the '86 party conferences.

Left CND's message tours the party conferences.

Below CND supporters demonstrate at the SDP conference in Harrogate. Nuclear matters dominated the discussions at all the party conferences.

Left Plans for new dock facilities for Britain's Trident submarines led to the Ministry of Defence taking over large tracts of hillside around Faslane and Coulport. At the request of Scottish activists, CND planned an ambitious mass civil disobedience which they called 'Reclaim the hills'.

Dire warnings were issued about the need for survival kits, thermos flasks and first aid, but in the event the weather was unusually mild, and the thousands who trespassed had a pleasant and uneventful day.

Bottom left Welsh groups stage a 'die-in' in the main shopping precinct in Cardiff in a series of actions drawing attention to the role of ROF Llanishen in the manufacture of the British bomb.

Right The Welsh national banner.

Below 'Hands across Scotland'. On 5th October 1986, a human chain was formed to stretch across the whole width of Scotland.

The event was organized by Parents for Survival, and was supported by over 70 national organizations. The organizers described it as 'a symbol of the hand of friendship extended between East and West, and a demonstration of the desire to stop the arms race'.

Top On 22nd and 23rd November 1986, continuing the 'British bomb' theme of decentralized action, CND supporters demonstrated the links between nuclear power stations, nuclear waste and nuclear weapons at Sellafield.

Above and opposite A week later CND scored a media success when television companies took up the story of the nuclear convoy routes, drawing to people's attention the fact that nuclear materials were regularly passing through residential areas.

Protest army sets out to expose A-convoys

AS THOUSANDS of CND protesters set out yesterday on a national day of action to expose secret nuclear convoys, a senior Tory MP said that in wartime they would be shot.

"They would not only be committing treason, they would be liable to be shot," said Gerry Neale, the new chairman of Tories for Defence and Multilateral Disarmament.

by ANDREW MOGER

The anti-nuclear organisers said up to 25,000 support- lision could detonate conven-

months. And they fear a col-

in the

ent has f secrecy nents of nuclear ND chair- We have ffold and g it. nt chil- nuclear millions television t."

ansporta- m bomb f Defence if plans s subma- tiple-war- ahead in

g for Po- isewatch

lightin help a possib "The know nuclea said M

Others mount vigils along the and country lane say are used to siles, spent fuel submarines and active material.

Organisers clai cking network 120 convoys in

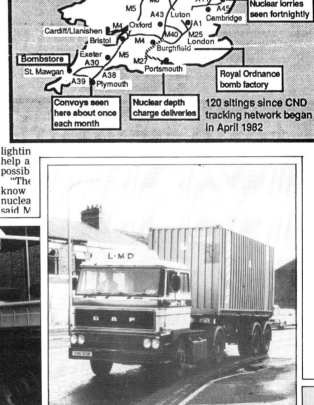

The Convoy Routes

- ▬▬ New route
- ── Repeated sitings of convoy
- 〜〜〜 At least one siting

Missile store for Polaris submarines

Coulport

Glasgow

M8

M6 A1

Newcastle

Carlisle

A66

Scotch Corner A1

Former Army barracks used as overnight stop. Convoy sited once, in August

Liverpool

M6 A1

M1 Leicester

Overnight stop

Birmingham

M6

A47 Marham

Honington

A11

Nuclear lorries seen fortnightly

M5

A43 Luton

A45 Cambridge

Cardiff/Llanishen

M4 Oxford

A1

Bristol

M4 M40 M25 London

Bombstore

Exeter M5 Burghfield

A30 M27

St. Mawgan

Portsmouth

A39 A38 Plymouth

Royal Ordnance bomb factory

Convoys seen here about once each month

Nuclear depth charge deliveries

120 sitings since CND tracking network began in April 1982

Top A Polaris warhead convoy on the M6, travelling from the Faslane submarine base in Scotland to ROF Burghfield in Berkshire.

Above A flask of spent fuel from the Magnox reactor at Hinkley Point nuclear power station is transported through Bridgewater in Somerset.

Above right Uranium on its way to BNFL Springfields, photographed in Preston.

Meanwhile Cruisewatch was becoming more and more proficient. A convoy on exercise was effectively ambushed on 4th November 1986 *(opposite)* while another convoy was brought to a halt by demonstrators on 25th November *(below)*.

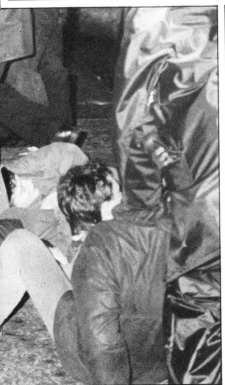

IT COSTS MILLIONS.
IT KILLS MILLIONS.
AND IT'S COMING DOWN
YOUR STREET.

Nuclear weapons could cost us the Earth.
We're better off without them.

CND

The year ended with good news for one CND supporter. Farmer David Barbour painted a huge yellow CND symbol on his barn roof, directly under the flight path of and clearly visible to the American pilots on exercise from the USAF base at Upper Heyford. The local authority told him to remove it, saying it was against planning regulations, but David Barbour appealed to the Secretary of State for the Environment – and won.

1987 opened with an event which had been long predicted by anti-nuclear campaigners – an accident involving nuclear weapons in transit.

It was not the first accident involving nuclear weapons. That happened in 1956 when an American bomber crashed into a nuclear bomb store at Lakenheath. But unlike the first accident which was an official secret for 26 years, the events of 10th January 1987 were dramatically covered by all the media, which accepted CND's statement that the vehicle involved was carrying nuclear weapons.

Here armed soldiers throw a mile-square cordon around the scene of the accident, where one lorry ended up on its side and a second was hanging over a ditch.

The Ministry of Defence, following normal practice, would neither confirm nor deny the presence of nuclear weapons, but experts believe the lorries were carrying nuclear depth charges from Royal Navy ships at Portsmouth to be serviced at ROF Burghfield. The recovery operation took 18 hours.

WHAT NEXT?

As the events of 1987 unfold and this book goes to press, only one thing is certain – CND will continue to work for nuclear disarmament.

Throughout its near 30-year history, the Campaign for Nuclear Disarmament has maintained a consistent, non-aligned, principled stand against all nuclear weapons. Now, in the 1980s, it has finally broken the political consensus that existed around British nuclear weapons policy for 40 years. Membership (local and national) is estimated at some 250,000, 180 local authorities have adopted and practise a nuclear-free declaration, and 29 major trade unions, representing six million people, have affiliated to CND.

Nuclear disarmament today is not only a party-political debate, it involves many facets of society. It has drawn substantial support from doctors, nurses, the clergy, scientists, teachers, artists, musicians and even retired military officers. Journalists, film-makers and civil servants have all exposed and implicitly condemned the secrecy of nuclear war-planning, and over the past six years more than 10,000 people have been arrested for acts of civil disobedience.

Without doubt millions of people in both East and West share a conscious desire for nuclear disarmament and an end to the cold war. As a result political controversy has surrounded every new development in the nuclear arms race, while its escalation has continued unabated.

Following the collapse of the US-USSR Reykjavic summit in November 1986, prospects for nuclear disarmament looked grim. The Soviet Union ended its unilateral moratorium on nuclear testing at the end of the year, while President Reagan boosted 'Star Wars' research, breached the SALT II Treaty and became embroiled in the 'Irangate' controversy. It looked as though the Reykjavic vision of a nuclear-free world had finally died.

However, at the beginning of March 1987, Mikhail Gorbachev's unexpected proposals for the removal of all intermediate nuclear weapons from Europe transformed the international situation.

To remove cruise, Pershing IIs and SS20s from Europe would be the first actual reduction of nuclear weapons in history – a subtle acknowledgment of the uselessness of such weapons for defence, and of the greater security that could derive from their removal. It would also provide a powerful precedent for further nuclear disarmament, and proof that unilateral initiatives can lead to multilateral agreements.

Whatever the outcome, however, five nuclear-armed states will still hold the world hostage to the ultimate holocaust. They bear an awesome responsibility, only matched by the peoples of the peace movements, whose struggle for nuclear disarmament continues apace.

TIME CHART

1905	Einstein proposes the theory of Special Relativity, $E = mc^2$.
1919	Rutherford demonstrates how the nucleus breaks down when bombarded with alpha particles.
1931	Einstein urges scientists to refuse military work.
1938	Hahn and Strassman discover nuclear fission in uranium.
1939	3rd September. World War II begins.
1942	13th August. Manhattan project in the USA, to develop atomic weapons. 12th December. Fermi produces the first controlled chain reaction in a nuclear pile.
1945	May. End of World War II in Europe. 16th July. USA tests the world's first atomic weapon, at Alamogordo in the New Mexico desert. Atomic scientist Leo Szilard and colleagues protest against the use of the bomb. 6th August. US airforce drops atom bomb on Hiroshima. 9th August. A second atomic bomb is dropped on Nagasaki. 2nd September. End of World War II.
1946	Plaid Cymru adopts a policy of opposition to all nuclear weapons. Spaatz-Tedder agreement establishes US bases in Britain.
1949	24th August. Ten West European states, including Britain, join Canada and USA in forming the North Atlantic Treaty Organization (NATO). 22nd September. Soviet Union explodes its first atomic bomb.
1950	100 Cambridge scientists petition the British government to halt atomic weapons development. British Peace Committee collects a million signatures for the Stockholm Peace Appeal. 30th November. President Truman threatens to use atomic bombs against the Communists during the Korean war.
1952	11th January. Peace Pledge Union organizes the first British protest against nuclear weapons. 1st March. First demonstration at Aldermaston against the British bomb. 3rd October. First British atomic bomb exploded off north-west coast of Australia.
1954	1st March. US test first H-bomb in Pacific. 23rd September. Death of Japanese fisherman caused by fallout from the H-bomb test. National H-bomb Committee formed in Britain. Coventry City Council disbands its Civil Defence Committee.
1955	Gertrude Fishwick sets up Golders Green Committee for the Abolition of Nuclear Weapons Tests. 5th May. West Germany joins NATO. 14th May. Seven East European states, including East Germany, join the USSR to form the Warsaw Treaty Organization.
1956	Suez crisis. Hungarian uprising. 23rd April. Soviet H-bomb announced.

1957	7th February. National Campaign Against Nuclear Weapons Tests (NCANWT) formed. 12th May. NCANWT organizes a women's protest march. 15th May. First British H-bomb test. 7th October. Massive radioactive discharges occur following a fire at Windscale where plutonium for bombs is manufactured. Nye Bevan opposes unilateral nuclear disarmament at the Labour Party conference.
1958	17th February. Launch meeting of the Campaign for Nuclear Disarmament. 22nd February. US supplies 60 Thor atomic missiles to UK. CND's first march from London to Aldermaston. Liberal Party Assembly votes against Britain's own nuclear weapons.
1959	October. Harold Macmillan leads Conservative Party to its third successive election victory.
1960	2nd January. Direct Action Committee Against Nuclear War blockades Harrington missile base. 13th February. First French atomic test in Algeria. Labour Party conference votes in favour of unilateral nuclear disarmament. 25th October. Committee of 100 is launched.
1961	18th February. First major civil disobedience action by Committee of 100 at the Ministry of Defence. March. First US nuclear submarine (Polaris) enters Holy Loch, Scotland. Berlin Wall is built. 17th September. 15,000 take part in banned Committee of 100 demonstration in Trafalgar Square.
1962	100,000 people attend the Easter Rally at the end of CND's Aldermaston march. 13th July. Committee of 100 members demonstrate in Moscow. 22nd October. Cuba missile crisis. 21st December. UK purchase of American Polaris missiles announced.
1963	12th April. 'Spies for Peace' reveal location of regional Seats of Government bunkers for use in nuclear war. Scottish Nationalists vote against all nuclear weapons and bases. 6th August. Partial Test Ban Treaty is signed, banning nuclear weapons tests in atmosphere, outer space and under water.
1965	12th March. First major demonstration against Vietnam war.
1966	First (unofficial) showing of Peter Watkins' film, *The War Game,* made for the BBC but then banned. Harold Wilson leads Labour Party to general election victory.
1967	Outer Space Treaty, banning nuclear weapons in earth's orbit and stationing in outer space.
1968	18th March. Biggest ever British demonstration against the Vietnam war. Non-Proliferation Treaty signed, banning transfer of nuclear weapons technology outside the five nuclear weapon states and committing the latter to halt the arms race. France and China refuse to sign. 20th August. Soviet Union invades Czechoslovakia.
1970	Edward Heath wins British general election for the Conservatives.

1972	ABM Treaty between US and USSR limits anti-ballistic missile systems. SALT I Interim Agreement places agreed ceilings on ballistic missile launchers of USA and USSR. Labour Party conference votes in favour of unilateral nuclear disarmament, but policy is ignored in practice.
1974	October. Labour Party wins general election by a small margin then calls and wins a second general election. 13th November. Karen Silkwood, US nuclear industry employee, is murdered as she tries to expose malpractice at her workplace.
1977	Liberal Party conference votes against nuclear power. 19th March. Huge march in Amsterdam against US production of the neutron bomb (expected to be deployed in Europe but later cancelled by President Carter).
1979	SALT II Treaty signed by Carter and Brezhnev, placing limits on the developments of strategic nuclear weapons. 28th March. A nuclear power plant at Three Mile Island, Harrisburg, USA approaches melt-down in a near catastrophic accident. 3rd May. Margaret Thatcher leads the Conservatives to power in Britain. Ronald Reagan is elected President of the United States. 12th December. NATO announces that 572 American cruise and Pershing II missiles are to be sited in Western Europe. 26th December. Soviet Union invades Afghanistan. President Reagan announces he will not ratify SALT II Treaty.
1980	February. European Nuclear Disarmament (END) founded. 17th June. British government announce the cruise missile sites, and their intention to buy Trident. Labour Party conference overwhelmingly backs unilateral nuclear disarmament. 26th October. 80,000 people take part in CND rally against cruise and Trident. 15th November. Manchester declares itself a nuclear-free zone.
1981	Social Democratic Party (SDP) is formed. TUC conference votes for unilateral nuclear disarmament. 5th September. Women for Life on Earth set up a peace camp at RAF Greenham Common. Liberal Party Assembly votes to oppose cruise missiles. Scottish National Party votes to secede from NATO policy. Biggest ever CND demonstration held in London. 500,000 people demonstrate in West Germany. 15th November. Thousands of American women encircle the Pentagon. 21st November. 350,000 march against nuclear weapons in the Netherlands. British government suspends nuclear waste disposal drilling at 20 sites after massive protests.
1982	23rd February. Wales becomes a nuclear-free zone. Mid Glamorgan County Council abandons building of bunker. 6th June. At the height of the Falklands war, 250,000 people demonstrate in London against nuclear weapons. Home Office announces cancellation of major civil defence exercise 'Hard Rock'. 12th June. 800,000 people demonstrate in New York against nuclear weapons. 19th June. 1,000 Kwojelain Atoll landowners occupy key islands in the Pacific to protest against nuclear weapons tests. 2nd July. First European Nuclear Disarmament convention held in Brussels. 10th November. Brezhnev dies. Andropov is appointed his successor. 30,000 women 'embrace the base' at Greenham Common to protest against cruise deployment.

1983	23rd March. The beginning of 'Star Wars'. President Reagan makes a speech about space defence against nuclear weapons.
	1st April. CND organizes a 14-mile human chain linking RAF Greenham Common with AWRE Aldermaston and ROF Burghfield.
	The Church and the Bomb published.
	9th June. Margaret Thatcher's government re-elected.
	Foreign Office clerk, Sarah Tisdall, leaks memo concerning arrival of cruise missiles to *The Guardian* newspaper.
	December. First flight of cruise missiles arrives at Greenham Common.
1984	Andropov dies and is replaced by Chernenko.
	14th April. Nationwide demonstrations by CND at over 100 American bases and facilities.
	9th June. Massive CND demonstration during the visit of US President Ronald Reagan.
	September. Ten-day protest at Greenham attracts women from all over the world.
	27th October. CND holds major demonstration against Trident at Barrow.
	Ronald Reagan is re-elected President of the USA.
1985	6th February. 1,500 soldiers remove peace campaigners from RAF Molesworth in night raid.
	11th March. Chernenko dies and Mikhail Gorbachev becomes the new leader of the Soviet Union.
	Soviet Union begins unilateral moratorium on nuclear testing on 6th August, the 40th anniversary of the bombing of Hiroshima.
	CND sit-down in Moscow in support of Moscow Group for Trust members.
	In a surprise reversal of policy, the British Labour Party votes against nuclear power.
	26th October. Rally for the Human Race. CND links disarmament and development in major rally.
	November. Ronald Reagan and Mikhail Gorbachev hold a summit meeting in Geneva.
1986	6th February. 6,000 people blockade RAF Molesworth.
	15th April. US strike aircraft bomb Libya from British bases. Massive protests follow.
	17th April. CND launches a major public information campaign on its 'basic case' for unilateral nuclear disarmament.
	26th April. The world's worst nuclear accident to date occurs at Chernobyl nuclear power station in the USSR.
	8th July. CND lobby against Star Wars.
	29th July. CND takes the British government to court over phone-tapping.
	The autumn conferences of all the major opposition parties are dominated by nuclear debates. The Liberal Party rejects a common approach with the SDP over the 'Eurobomb'.
	4th October. Thousands take part in civil disobedience at Coulport, and even greater numbers link hands to form a chain across Scotland.
	11th October. The Soviet Union initiates a mini-summit at Reykjavic in which unprecedented cuts in nuclear weapons are discussed by Reagan and Gorbachev.
	4th November. Cruisewatch stops cruise convoy on exercise.
	'Irangate' crisis breaks in USA, revealing covert arms sales to Iran.
	December. SALT II Treaty is breached by USA.
	Soviet Union announces it will end the moratorium on nuclear testing unless US responds.
1987	5th January. US undertakes another nuclear test.
	26th February. USSR carries out its first nuclear test for 18 months.
	28th February. Gorbachev proposes an agreement to remove all intermediate nuclear weapons from Europe.

ACKNOWLEDGMENTS

The author wishes to thank John Cox and Diana Shelley for their help with the text, and Carol Moody for typing it.

Reference sources used were as follows: *Overkill* by John Cox (Penguin, 1977), *Left, Left, Left* by Peggy Duff (Allison & Busby, 1971), *The CND Story* edited by John Minnion/Philip Bolsover (Allison & Busby, 1983), *Protest and Survive* edited by E. P. Thompson/Dan Smith (Penguin, 1980), *The Unsinkable Aircraft Carrier* by Duncan Campbell (Michael Joseph, 1984).

The author and publishers would also like to thank the following for their kind permission to reproduce copyright illustrations:
Associated Press: *67t.* Carlos Augusto/I.F.L: *58t.* John Birdsall Photography: *84* © Murdo Mcleod, *94t, 111tl.* Birmingham Post & Mail: *68t.* David Blackburn: *120b.* Martin Bond: *54tl. 54tr, 71t, 98b, 133c, 133bl, 133br.* Howard Bowcott: *131t.* Stefano Cagnoni/I.F.L: *66t, 73tr, 103t, 105t.* Camera Press: *30, 46t, 80b, 108tl, 111tr.* John Chapman: *123b, 124.* CND Archive: *5, 7, 8, 17b, 22b, 24t, 24b, 29t, 29b, 33 Maurice Rickards, 35t John Hopkins, 35b, 37tr, 39, 44t, 44b, 49, 56b, 67b, 68b, 70b M. Humby, 75tr, 82b, 93b, 102t, 112t, 119t, 119b, 120t, 126, 129t, 135b.* CND Cymru: *61.* Donald Cooper: *45t.* Creative Photography Ltd: *42-3.* Daily Mail: *75tl, 88tl, 88b.* Daily Star: *89t.* East Anglian Daily Times: *132t.* Barbara Egglestone: *78t, 93t.* Evening Standard: *91b, 92t.* Melanie Friend: *front cover, 94b/Format, 95t, 96b, 97b, 106b, 107t, 110, 111b, 112b, 113t, 113b, 115b, 125, 127b, 130t, 132b.* John Frost Historical Newspaper Service: *31t Daily Mirror, 47tl Los Angeles Herald Examiner, 50b, 103b Evening Standard, 116t, 122 Sunday Mirror, 123t, 123c.* Tony Gay: *53.* Mary Giles: *130b.* Glasgow Herald & Evening Times: *45b, 78b.* Glasgow & Strathclyde Council: *54bl, 54br.* Henry Grant Collection/Museum of London: *9, 10t, 10b, 12tl, 12br, 13, 14, 15, 16tl, 16br, 17t, 18t, 18b, 19, 20-1, 22tr, 25, 26t, 27b, 28, 32b, 36t, 36b, 81t.* Sheila Gray/Format: *98t.* Sally & Richard Greenhill: *52b, 54c, 63t, 92c, 108tr, 127t.* Greenpeace: *82t.* The Guardian: *27t, 40, 50t British Library; 86b, 90t Camera Press.* Mike Haley: *121t.* Ian Hargreaves: *129b.* John Harris/I.F.L: *115b, 136-7.* Peter Harrop/Report: *41.* Tessa Howland/I.F.L.: *58b.* Pam Isherwood/Format: *73b, 83t, 83b.* John Kent: *77r.* Jenny Matthews/Format: *63b, 74t, 79t.* Rick Matthews/I.F.L: *69, 114.* Paul Mattsson/Frame: *116b.* Pete Maxey: *105bl, 106t, 118t/I.F.L., 118b/I.F.L., 127c.* Steve McGrady: *65t.* Medical Campaign Against Nuclear Weapons: *55.* David Modell: *117b.* Maggie Murray/Format: *73cr, 79b.* Bob Naylor: *107b, 134, 135t.* Newbury Weekly News: *52t.* NICND: *80t, 92b.* Joanne O'Brien/Format: *85.* Eamonn O'Dwyer/I.F.L.: *47tr.* Raissa Page/Format: *72t.* Peace News: *11, 23, 37tl Graham Keen.* Photosource: *22tl.* Popperfoto: *38.* Press Asociation: *34t, 37b, 138.* Brenda Prince/Format: *72b, 100t.* Rex: *60, 64b, 95b, 108-9.* SCND: *26b, 31b, 99t.* The Scotsman: *32t British Library, 131b.* Martin Shakeshaft/I.F.L: *97t.* David V. Sinden: *51b.* John Smith/I.F.L: *74b.* South Wales Argus: *65b.* Laurie Sparham/I.F.L: *46b.* Derek Speirs/I.F.L: *47b.* Sun Newspapers: *88tr, 89b.* Telegraph Newspapers: *86t, 91tl.* The Times Newspapers: *24c, 34b, 77l, 87, 90b.* TUCND: *121c, 121b.* Prudence de Villiers: *56t.* Andrew Wiard/Report: *51t, 57, 62, 64t, 70t, 75b, 81b, 99b, 104t, 104b, 117.* WMCND: *105cr.* Chris Wormald: *101c, 101b.*

Picture research by Diana Morris.
Design by Patrick Nugent.